SEMIOTEXT(E) INTERVENTION SERIES

Published by Semiotext(e)
PO BOX 629, South Pasadena, CA 91031
www.semiotexte.com

Special thanks to Noura Wedell and Juliana Halpert

Design: Hedi El Kholti
Cover image: Lauren Mackler

ISBN: 978-1-63590-168-9
Distributed by the MIT Press, Cambridge, Mass.,
and London, England
Printed in the United States of America
10 9 8 7 6 5 4 3 2

Tiziana Terranova

After the Internet

Digital Networks between
Capital and the Common

semiotext(e)
intervention
series □ 33

Contents

Introduction

(2022)

Before the 2020s brought the world to a (temporary) sudden halt with the first taste of a truly planetary epidemic right before it reignited the fuse of a potential nuclear world war, there were the 2010s–the accelerationist years. The second decade of the 21st century witnessed the precipitous crystallization of a massive worldwide infrastructure—one that has brought together technologies of communication and computation, connection and calculation in unprecedented ways. The infrastructure which today constitutes the dominant manifestation of digital connectivity does not seem to be quite what previous decades called "the internet," rather, it appears as a complex of privately owned online services that call themselves "platforms."[1] This Corporate Platform Complex (CPC) is currently ruled by a handful of very large and powerful companies (also known as Big Tech) bearing names such as Google/Alphabet, Amazon,

Apple, Facebook/Meta, Microsoft, Alibaba and Tencent. Indeed, so powerful has the Corporate Platform Complex grown that the pandemic has actually acted like a booster in relation to it. In 2020 and 2021, while the global economy shrank significantly overall, the CPC's wealth soared as those who were confined at home or restricted in movement found themselves relying more than ever on digital connectivity. Indeed, not only did the so-called digital surge of 2020 made Big Tech richer overall, but it opened up new markets (video-conferencing, distance learning), and emboldened ever more expansive dreams. The Metaverse initiative, for example, launched by the company formerly known as Facebook in 2021, aims to make the pandemic experience of learning, working, socializing and playing at a distance an ordinary one—envisioning a future crypto-economic, Pixar-like augmented/virtual world, where the digital and the real become perceptually indistinguishable.

The shift from the internet to the CPC can be seen at work in the technological, economic and cultural transformations of digital networking that significantly depart from the internet as we used to know it. Overall, there has been a significant shift from the internet as a set of interoperable network protocols governed by a series of public and/or voluntary non-profit organizations, to gated digital communities with strong ownership of data, software and infrastructure. Technically, the CPC has moved away from the symbolic centrality of peer-to-peer architectures towards a much stronger centrality of cloud computing corresponding to the shift from desktop to mobile devices. Automation has also been largely expanded in ways that make active use of data generated by users' participation—a crucial move in the regeneration of the artificial intelligence program currently at work in machine learning.

The economic transformation of digital networking is also starkly evident, as a technological infrastructure that mostly supported public or nonprofit uses has transmogrified into a gigantic business and industrial milieu characterized by high degrees of concentration. A close relationship with financial capital (from angel investors to venture capital to financial markets proper after the initial public offerings) is needed to get a foothold in the race for continuous disruption of existing markets (for example, transport, tourism, and food delivery). Network effects enable the successful platforms to create monopolies that support "ecosystems" composed by a multitude of smaller economic agents who completely depend for their sustenance on the larger actors—a model spearheaded by Google's AdSense and AdWords programs, but which is now ubiquitous and epitomized by Amazon Marketplace, the Android Play and Apple App stores but also by companies such as Uber and Airbnb.

From the point of view of network culture, the figure of the typical "subject" has also changed. The "user as master of the machine" or as "homesteading pioneer of the electronic frontier" has (unregretfully) waned, but what has waxed in its place is also not quite reassuring. The consensus seems to be that the user has morphed from master to addict, as behaviorist interfaces that are designed with the purpose of maximizing engagement corrupt collective intelligence by facilitating the spread of fake news, conspiracy theories, and hate speech.[2] Instead of the hacker, the "influencer" has become the new heroic figure, the focus of subjectivation. Against the threat of the Multitude as a figure of difference and heterogeneity, the ghost of the People has also raised its head again—ephemerally united but most of the time polarized and divided, when not engaged in downright nationalist warfare against or engaged in building barriers against the threat of Other People(s).[3]

According to Hito Steyerl, as a result of this process, what is still sometimes called the internet has lost its previous meanings, that is, it has "stopped being a possibility"—something new and exciting that promised a better future.[4] It has become a *residual* technology, still "an effective element of the present," but less legible and intelligible than it used to be. It continues to exist, but interstitially, in ways that are almost hardly ever perceptible to those large and powerful entities that have overtaken it.[5] Standards and protocols developed as part of the project of creating the internet as a public and open network still operate, but they are increasingly buried under a thick layer of corporate ones. The internet's own native subcultures, such as those that formed in the 1980s and 1990s, have gone underground, assembling in the so-called dark web, in IRC chats, in some forums, in pirate file-sharing networks, in websites with no social plugins, in mesh networks and wikis, and maybe also in the chaotic informational milieus of some secure, encrypted, open source messaging apps.

Reaching out with their data-mining tentacles, the new owners of the digital world have, as Marxists might say, *subsumed* the internet, that is, transmuted, encompassed, incorporated it, but not necessarily beaten or dissolved it. As a subsumed entity, the internet is not so much dead as undead, a ghostly presence haunting the Corporate Platform Complex with the specters of past hopes and potentials. Thus, whereby the CPC displays an increasing concentration of control, the specter of the internet persists as a much more muted, but perceptible aspiration towards an unprecedented distribution of the power to know, understand, coordinate and decide. While platforms ask us to accept contracts ("terms and conditions") that bestow upon them the sovereign power to shut down, expel, ban and cancel those who do not comply with them, the specter of the internet remains as the possibility to connect through technical forms that do not transfer ownership of data or control of use. As platforms enforce a strict asymmetry between servers and clients, the internet insists that all nodes can be peer. In contrast to the degradation of public debate for the sake of measurable engagement caused by the CPC, the ghost of the internet whispers of the possibility of new types of collective intelligence. And while the platform economy turns digital labor into casual and precarious work, the undead internet insists on the superiority of commons-based production over proprietary accumulation of capital and of social (ethical, existential, aesthetic) values over the imperium of monetization or exchange value.

A Much-Abridged History of Networks

The rise of the CPC can be seen as part of a new turn in the much longer history of networks, characterized by an unprecedented and accelerated integration of communication and computation, that is, the capacity to connect and pass on and to calculate and reason. This new turn explicitly mobilizes what can be described as the three main properties of networks: their being constituted historically as comprising abstract mathematical symbols, observable empirical objects, and engineered artificial systems. As an abstract mathematical indexical sign, the network is the domain of the field of graph theory. The abstract figure of the network is the *graph*—"a mathematical object consisting of points, also called *vertices*, or *nodes*, and lines, also called *edges* or *links*, which abstracts away all the details... except for... connectivity"—the most successful and oldest example of that *analysis situ*, or geometry of situations, which was wished for by Gottfried Leibniz as a geometrical formalization of relational space.[6] Network graphs imply the fundamental property of connectedness or continuity which thus becomes calculable or computable. For network scientists, this mathematical object manifests itself in observable empirical objects (as in social or biological networks) that act as mediums for the transmission of information, and tend to "arise naturally, in a manner that is typically unplanned and decentralized," and which can be studied (that is their properties can be calculated) by using the tools of graph theory.[7] For network scientists, these empirical networks also include *engineered* or *artificial* networks which, albeit "intended to serve a single, coordinated purpose (transportation, power delivery, communications) ...

are built over long periods of time by many independent agencies and authorities."[8]

Perhaps networks are not ready-made entities that science was just waiting to find out about, as Fredrich Kittler once argued, but the mathematization of networks started in relation to the problem of diagramming physical movement across one such engineered network—as in the puzzle of Königsberg's bridges which marked the first mathematical formulation of graph theory in 1736 and concerned the systems of bridges connecting the different parts of this Northern European estuary town.[9] While street and road networks undoubtedly constitute a very important example of engineered networks, communication systems are as important—and have become with time increasingly so. While it is always possible for a physical network of streets, roads and bridges to double as a communication network in as much as it can be used to transport information, the latter also has its own distinct history—one that entails the abstraction and codification of information as a transmissible signal. One of its earliest examples could be the system of watchtowers assembled during the Islamic Golden Age in the ninth century A.D. which were said to be capable of transmitting a message across the 2640 miles that separated the coastal Egyptian city of Alexandria from the Spanish/Moroccan city of Ceuta in just one day.[10]

Since the 19th century, communication networks have operated at the speed of electrical and/or electromagnetic signals traveling through cables or through the air—as with telegraphy, telephony, radio and television. As a type of electrical network, digital networks depend on electricity as well. However, unlike telegraphy, telephony or television, they present the unique feature of being composed by logical machines that can use micro-transistors to compute any function or activity which can be coded through programming languages as a series of executable instructions or algorithms. This is arguably related to the fact that contemporary digital networks are the first communication networks in history to deploy computational devices as nodes.

The systematic integration of communication and computation, while implicit in the network as an abstract and empirical object, actually becomes explicit at the point when computers start to be used to communicate—and not just to calculate. The first use of computers to communicate can be traced back to the practice of time-sharing in the 1960s, when different users could access the same large machine to send and receive messages to each other—indeed this was the time when the user was constituted and named as such as a way to make time spent with the machine accountable.[11] The first computer network whereby different machines in different locations could communicate to each other was ARPANET—a wide-area, packet-switched network connecting computing centers affiliated with the Advanced Research Projects Agency of the United States Department of Defense. Launched in 1969, ARPANET was shut down in 1983.

Unlike ARPANET, the internet is not just a computer network but *a network of computer networks* (literally an inter-network). Hence its inception might be more appropriately dated back to the implementation of the so-called internet protocols, such as TCP/IP in the 1970s. The internet not only made computers capable of communicating with each other *locally* but implemented a logical and technical infrastructure which allowed *different computer networks* to smoothly connect to each other even over large distances. In the internet, computation and communication for the first time operated together as part of an architecture that was built to scale across differences, that is, to expand.[12]

Between the 1980s and 1990s, computer networks such as the internet but also other types of more local ones were circumscribed enough to host their own very distinct subcultures. The hegemonic social subjects of the internet technocultures were notoriously (mostly) white male nerds. On the internet, as Lisa Nakamura pointed out, the default identity was white and male, albeit dominated by pseudonymity (as in IRC channels) rather than anchored to authenticated proper names as in today's Corporate Platform Complex.[13] Those who identified with the hacker ethos relied on and built free and open source social software such as email, messaging, file transfer protocols, WAIS and gopher, and UNIX newsgroups. Politically, early digital cultures were pretty much dominated by two main tendencies. On the one hand, the white (mostly North American) cyber-libertarians emanating from the 1960s countercultures who maintained that information wanted to be free, subscribed to Declarations of Independence of Cyberspace, "homesteaded" on the "Electronic Frontier," and watched out against all attempts to limit the freedom of the "pioneers of virtual communities."[14] On the other hand, the white (mostly European, mostly male) radicals identifying with the DIY anarchist ethos of the punk and squatters' movements from the 1980s, who believed that computer networks could foster new kinds of autonomous forms of political organization.[15] Local networks, such as Bulletin Board Systems, existed alongside the internet, but used similar technologies to connect to each other (as in Fidonet). In spite of a clear hegemony of white, male subjects, however, the internet also hosted some rambunctious counter-hegemonic, minoritarian and oppositional cultures (as in feminist/queer groups, Asian and black technocultures).[16]

The end of the internet was precipitated by the lifting of the ban on commercial use in 1991 by the US government, in a period when the so-called "information superhighway" was the bipartisan buzzword of US politicians. When in 1993, CERN (the European Organization for Nuclear Research) put the World Wide Web software assembled by one of its engineers, Tim Berners-Lee, in the public domain, the WWW user-friendly visual interface was immediately taken up by commerce. The first wave of internet business took its name from the new web domains assigned to commercial use, that is "dot-coms." In the late 1990s, the dot-coms had represented a real break with the old corporate culture of the computer industry, such as epitomized by the IBM behemoth. Their workforce was accurately described by one of its first ethnographers, Andrew Ross, as "no collar"—to mark its difference from the division between white and blue collar workers, that is, intellectual and manual labor, in the Fordist factory.[17] Like Apple, but at a smaller and wider scale, they borrowed from the 1960s counterculture but were more directly influenced by the US Ivy League university campus life. Features such as the predominance of informal hierarchies, a culture of work as play, an intense personalization of relationships were all due to have an enduring influence on the corporate platform complex. This was the period of formation of what Andy Cameron and Richard Barbrook called "the California ideology"—a term that exemplified for them a set of ideas and attitudes which spread out from the North American region of Silicon Valley to the world.[18] The dot-com wave peaked, crashed and burned in 2001, a few months before the terrorist attacks of September 11, as the collapse of the Nasdaq stock market marked the beginning of the "first internet recession."[19] The crash did not spell the end of the capitalist colonization of the internet, as some hoped, but was followed by a new, even more buoyant phase of commercialization that injected new capital into the development of technological innovations in ways that short-circuited and bypassed the slower processes of commons based networked peer production. Already in the mid-2000s, in fact, what was left of the internet industry was rallying back around the Web 2.0 banner—a term that identified the winners who had survived the collapse and which were to inspire a new wave of more successful business ventures.[20] The winning model involved the harnessing of the free labor of user participation, whose value was soon transmuted into the supposedly inert ore of the data mines stored in the anonymous bunker-like concrete blocks of server farms. The early platform economy thus could literally sail through the rough winds of the much larger and systemic financial storm of 2008—one that wreaked havoc on the more vulnerable households and nations, bringing foreclosures, repossessions and austerity as private corporate debt was shifted onto the shoulders of workers and nation states. In spite of the crash of 2008, in fact, wealth accumulated in the financial market and its power to over-determine the economy as a whole actually reached unprecedented levels in the 2010s—proportionate to its capacity to plunder the earth's resources as well as the products of social cooperation, which were channeled and shaped by the neo-monadological architecture of digital social networks. As Saskia Sassen points out, measures of the value of financial markets in 2014 involved the introduction of quantities such as "a quadrillion" (as compared to a global GDP of sixty trillion)—which included the assumed value of financial products such as derivatives.[21]

Most of today's corporate platform giants were thus literally hatched between *two* financial crises, the smaller, circumscribed one of 2001 and the more systemic, global one of 2008. At the same time, they could not have possibly achieved the current dominance of digital networking if they had not been able to draw on financial capital to sustain them in the sometimes quite long periods before large losses turned into big revenue. Companies like Google, Amazon and Facebook were part of this new breed of internet businesses that inherited some of the features of the working cultures of the dot-coms, but, wary of the debacle of their immediate predecessors, were much more aggressively oriented towards monetization. The CPC arose as a reaction to the crash of 2001 assuming the initial form of the "start-up"—a peculiar economic organization whose culture has been described by anthropologists and sociologists, narrated by novelists, depicted in films and TV series, chronicled by celebratory accounts but also painted in somber or lurid hues by disgruntled and disaffected ex-employees. Some of the characteristics of the start-up corporate culture that emerge from this plethora of studies and representations are: its youthful composition; the hyper-valorization of technical wizardry coded as male and the devaluation of linguistic, humanistic and social knowledges coded as female; its predominant whiteness colored by small doses of Asian-ness; the cult of the founder(s); the distinction between employees who own shares of the company and those who do not; and the demand for affective investment in the company's mission which it shares with most capitalist corporations, but which intensifies in specific ways. When successful, start-ups become "unicorns," that is, privately owned companies that are valued at over one billion US dollars.

In the 2010s, some start-ups harnessed network effects in such a way as to favor the consolidation of quasi-monopolies, dramatically raising barriers to entry in key new areas of development such as hardware, social networking, e-commerce, searching, streaming, and work. Only very few of the companies that used to be start-ups have made it to Big Tech status, that is, the most prominent and prestigious companies—such as Alphabet (Google), Apple, Amazon, Meta (Facebook), Microsoft, Baidu, Ali Baba, Tencent, Xiaomi and to a lesser extent also Netflix; Uber and Twitter. As leading members of the CPC, these companies have pioneered the use of open-source software for the purposes of private accumulation and heavily invested in cloud computing infrastruc-tures which they use for data mining and processing, with huge environmental fallout. Today, they rule over a multitude of micro-businesses and secondary markets which depend on them for their liveli-hood. Sometimes they cooperate with the military and governments to develop and deploy tech-nologies that are used to suppress dissent and target subjugated groups. More often, they try to accommodate their intrinsic drive for ever-rising profits with the increasing calls for regulation—as their expansion threatens to overtake key governmental functions. In China, they are, in particular, subjected to strict governmental control, but the tendency seems also more generally to be making their future grip on digital networking less certain than it might appear today.

As the process of subsumption of the internet proceeded relentlessly throughout the 2010s, however, so did the intensification of protesting. As Nick Dyer-Witheford points out, "metrics of transnational social unrest—incidences of protest-events, and polls showing dissatisfaction with governing regimes—have ticked upwards for several years, reaching a level not witnessed since the late 1960s."[22] This has not presented itself as much in the benevolent image of US technologies exporting democracy to the rest of the world as a much more tense and ambivalent process of unexpected and unaccounted for possibilities. The logistical and communicative capacity of the CPC has been repeatedly exploited and turned around by "the counter-logistics of the riot,", that is, "the self-organization of protestors; their ability to gather; respond to police attack; disperse and reassemble; supply themselves with gas masks, food, or barricade materials; make collective decisions on the fly amidst police attacks and street fighting; connect with other protests, across cities, regions, and borders."[23] Thus, "platform capitalism spawned riot platforms."[24] Riot and protest platforms appeared first in the anti-austerity cycle of struggles of 2008/2014 (including the uprisings in Greece, North Africa and the Middle East); in the planetary protests against gender and racial violence which bear names such as Black Lives Matter and Ni una menos; in the transnational wave of unrest of 2018/2019 (in France, Hong Kong, Chile, Catalonia, Lebanon, Iran, Iraq, Algeria, Cameroon, Chad, Congo, Myanmar and Ethiopia amongst other places); but also with the global demonstrations, marches and actions of environmental movements such as Fridays for Future and Extinction Rebellion.

The rise of the CPC has also been accompanied by a more general transformation of the ways struggles are started and conducted as part of the larger shift from, as Maurizio Lazzarato puts it, "the" (singular) class struggle of the 19th and early 20th century to the "class struggles" (in the plural) of the late 20th and early 21st century (such as inflected by feminist, anti-racist, queer, subaltern, and indigenous histories, practices, and perspectives).[25] This has manifested as an unprecedented capacity of workers, women, indigenous, Black, Brown, and LGBTQI+ people to connect, coordinate and organize through such new means—as well as by the reconfiguration of the tactics and strategies used by those in power to foreclose and disrupt such capacities. Everywhere, to adopt Stefano Harney and Fred Moten's expression, both *special* and *general antagonism(s)* proliferate and intensify: special antagonisms such as those generated by exploitation in the workplace, racism and sexism everywhere, the ongoing environmental catastrophes and war, but also a general antagonism or, in the terms favored by Brian Massumi, a general state of *unrest* that is never quite completely tamed or subdued.[26] The general state of unrest does not comprise only the revolt of subjugated social groups, but also the backlash of reactionary political forces. Increasingly, global networks are the means through which all kinds of riots are plotted and planned, including "radical riots and reactionary riots; riots and counter-riots; riots that contest capitalism's systemic violence and riots that reaffirm that violence," but also emancipatory and reactive speech, new openings and harsh backlashes as the "constant struggle for freedom" meets and sometimes even turns into "a fight for servitude" as if it were salvation.[27] The post-internet corporate platform complex is thus far from being a pacified empire; it is agitated by a deep state of unrest. While on the one hand it seems as if it has colonized the world, one must also not forget that it is also somehow itself permanently *surrounded*.[28]

Between the Market and the Common(s)

In spite of the evident and undeniable displacement of the internet by the CPC, something which could be witnessed throughout the years that the essays that compose this book were written in, this is not a sad book. It is not, that is, a book dedicated to bemoaning the "rise and fall" of a promising new technology. It is thus neither a melancholic nor apocalyptic rumination, tinged by the affective tonality of nostalgia, mourning for that which no longer is, denouncing the hopelessness of the present, and warning against even worse catastrophes to come. The story of enclosure and capture that constitutes the common critical discourse on contemporary digital connectivity is only part of the story. The 2010s were not just the years of real subsumption of the internet, as Marxists might put it, but also years where a certain tension could still be grasped between different potential visions of a world permeated by digital networking. The process of subsumption implicated a whole series of potentials and conflicts that have been partially muted, but far from obliterated. In the 2010s, these potentials and conflicts presented themselves as a tension between, on the one hand, the power of the capitalist market and, on the other hand, the potential of the *Common*—a political concept that over the last decade in particular functioned as a rallying point for those who held on to a different vision of what computational connectivity could be. There is no wish to go back to the old internet, then, but for the possibility of a different kind of social imaginary for contemporary digital networks. Coming to terms with such possibility involves an updating of the Marxian analysis of capital in light of the innovation represented by the platform economy—a process that is well underway in a number of studies that address the new types of labor conditions, but also the very mechanisms of extraction of surplus value at work in such settings.[29]

The takeover of the internet by the capitalist market presented platformization as progressive and revolutionary—a universally beneficial disruption of a previous social and economic order. This so-called progressive revolution, however, has turned out to be more of a *counter-revolution* which operated a *normalization* with relation to the exceptionality that had been claimed for the so-called digital economy in the late 1990s and early 2000s. A symptom of this change was undoubtedly the sudden popularity, in the early 2010s, of the notion of the attention economy— that is, the re-orientation of capitalist competition for scarce resources towards the scramble to capture users' limited attention span. Platforms have been very active in implementing behaviorist interfaces that incite dopamine-driven compulsive logging-in, checking, clicking, liking and so on in ways that harness participation to what Jodi Dean presciently called communicative capitalism's circuits of drive.[30] This drive towards maximization of engagement has played a crucial role in the production of new ordinary pathologies of the connected brain—manifesting as recurrent moral panic about the popularity of fake news and conspiracy theories, and generally about what is perceived as the degradation of public opinion and civil society.

It is important to point out, however, that this turn towards the attention economy and behaviorist interfaces was *preceded* by the exponential growth of internet usage since the early 2000s—a mass sharing, uploading, posting, and discussing of content that took place initially mostly by means of non-proprietary software. Platform capitalism can be seen as a reaction to the kind of mass participation that initially turned the early entrepreneurial enthusiasm for the digital economy into the worrisome possibility of digital socialism.[31] In the 2000s, the Free and Open Source software movement, Wikipedia and early nonprofit-oriented examples of crowdsourcing questioned one of the founding myths of contemporary economic thinking: that market economics was the only real efficient way to go when it came to coordinating individual actions. This was a thesis that had been specifically articulated against the favorite tool of socialist economic policies since the 1920s: central planning. The neoliberal critique of central planning posed that the market (and specifically market pricing) was vastly superior to socialist economies because of "its ability to enable complex forms of social coordination with little or no central planning."[32] As Dyer-Witheford put it, for Austrian school economists, the "market enacts a distributed, spontaneous and emergent, non-coercive plan—what [Friedrich] Hayek called the 'catallaxy.'"[33] The shadow of Hayek's catallaxy could easily be detected in the biological metaphors popular amongst the digital avant-garde of the 1990s to describe the ways in which the internet seemed to be able to work without any real centralized control agency. The liberal and neoliberal idea that the market produces a spontaneous order (or equilibrium) and that in order to replace it a postcapitalist economy needs to find some kind of equivalent form of coordination is something that can be found in a number of theorizations of the post-digital, pre-platform economy of the late 2000s and early 2010s. These speculations revisited the tradition of so-called "red cybernetics"—as in the history of Soviet computing narrated by Francis Spufford in his novel *Red Plenty: Inside the Fifties Soviet Dream* (2010), but also in Eden Medina's account of Project Cybersyn in *Cybernetic Revolutionaries: Technology and Politics in Allende's Chile* (2011). If the economy is a computer, which somehow the capitalist market can enact much more flexibly than the rigid socialist mode of planning, it was argued, maybe digital networks could actually allow for a solution to the socialist calculation debate which could make a socialist economy a viable option again. Socialist planning, however, has turned out not to need Hayek's catallaxy to become actual again—as the use of this classic socialist instrument by the Chinese Communist Party to govern China's platform economy has shown. As Cornelius Castoriadis once argued, real socialism turned out to be just another kind of capitalist economy.[34]

On the other hand, the notion of the common(s) did not point in the direction of digital socialism, but towards the possibility of escaping the double bind of *either* liberal *or* socialist economy, private *or* public property. Here the founding moment is not so much the socialist calculation debate of the 1920s, but something that goes even further back—which does not oppose socialism and capitalism so much as pre-modern and modern. Hearkening back to pre-capitalist times, the "tragedy of the commons" which Garrett Hardin described in terms of the failure of individuals to care for shared property, actually historically evokes the expropriation by means of enclosures of the shared land of European croppers and farmers, but especially the genocidal dispossession experienced by indigenous and aboriginal peoples.

The notion of the commons, then, experienced a revival in the 2000s and 2010s in ways that questioned Garrett Hardin's account about the viability of common regimes of property, while also expanding the concept to include the question of information, data, communication networks, social cooperation and digital participation. With relation to the so-called digital commons, the theme was declined in two different, but related ways. The first tendency drew on the re-evaluation of the value of the commons as a regime of property by scholars such as Elinor Olstrom, who worked from within the framework of institutional analysis. The second framework deployed the political concept of the Common as part of a Marxian analysis of the transformation of the capitalist mode of production, by extending the notion of the common to the domain of *living knowledges* and *social cooperation*. On the one hand, then, the Nobel prizewinner for economics Elinor Olstrom effectively countered one of the founding myths of mainstream economics (such as Garett Hardin's "tragedy of the commons" thesis) by showing that commons could actually be very efficient ways of organizing the management of certain kinds of natural resources.

On the other hand, post-workerist Marxists argued that the Common indicates not only a specific kind of resource to which the common regime of property applies, but also the living knowledges and forms of social cooperation that go into the production and reproduction of shared goods and forms of life. This intrinsic element of the commons, they argued, in the post-Fordist mode of production, actually comes to constitute the primary engine of the production of wealth and the target of expropriation.[35]

One can see these two declinations of the theme of the common(s) in different political interpretations of the role of the Common in the digitally networked mode of production such as Yochai Benkler's *The Wealth of Networks* (2006) and Michael Hardt and Antonio Negri's *Commonwealth* (2011). In the first case, that is *The Wealth of Networks*, Benkler deployed the institutional analysis framework, with its emphasis on the centrality of the specific nature of the good at stake, to theorize the possibility of a *commons-based peer production* in the networked economy. Benkler's book in particular can be read as a formalization of many arguments about the peculiarity of the digital economy that were articulated first in the 1990s. Taking as its starting point Roland Coase's essay "The Nature of the Firm" (1937), the book put forward a theory of the peer-to-peer commons-based mode of production that did not imply a return of socialism, but which was compatible with mainstream economics. Benkler thus extended Olstrom's notion of the common to information, knowledge and cultural production in digital networks. Commons-based peer production, he argued, was made possible by the nonrival properties of information as a commodity, which are constructed through an analogy to the natural commons. Since the 1990s, in fact, a refrain of commentators on the digital economy had repeatedly stated the fact that information can be shared without alienation of property—I can give you a copy of a file I hold in my computer and still maintain possession of mine. The peculiar character of information in economic terms is thus that of being a nonrival good, which unlike material goods such as cars or bottles, can be shared without loss and duplicated, thanks to digitization, at a cost that is close to zero. As copyright enforcers are well aware of, once the first copy of a digital artwork (film, tune, photo) is made, copying and distributing it costs next to nothing. This was the premise according to which legal scholars such as Lawrence Lessing argued that, once obsolete barriers such as copyright were removed, a new renaissance of free cultural creativity was going to be unleashed. Like Olstrom's natural commons, Benkler maintained that the digital commons showed evidence of efficient self-management outside the domain of market relations based in private property. Warding off the threat of digital socialism by explicitly evoking in its very title a liberal classic such as Adam Smith *The Wealth of Nations* (1776), Benkler drew on the evidence provided by open-source software, Wikipedia and early not-for-profit crowdsourcing endeavors to argue that a self-organizing nonmarket mode of production was possible—indeed it was an actual reality emerging for the first time in modern history at the cutting edge of the economy rather than a residual, marginal and backward exception to the hegemony of the market. Participation in the commons-based digital economy was not irrational, that is, it still involved some kind of utility—or satisfaction of a need which manifested as interest or motivation, but a different one than the one presupposed by the market, such as the motivation to work with others, to see one's value recognized by peers and so on. The features that were supposed to make intelligible, and hence real, the commons-based peer economy included: the centrality of information as a non-rival good; the close-to-zero cost of the reproduction of information; the low costs of access to the means of production (computers and digital connectivity); and evidence of catallaxy (the invisible hand of the social) that, like the market, harmoniously coordinated individual initiatives. This was a dream of a mass of free individuals motivated by personal rather than strictly economic interests, who thanks to the falling costs of fixed capital (machines) could finally engender an economy of peers freely producing and sharing abundance, outcompeting the market (or at least reining it in), by creating a new economic zone where social rather than strictly economic motivations could find a new role. In particular, Benkler was very emphatic not to question the model of human nature that grounded economic theory in a specific vision of the subject, such as "methodological individualism," and its correlate—rational choice theory. As Caribbean scholar Sylvia Wynter might put it, the cosmogony of *homo oeconomicus* (or what she calls Man2) permeated this model of the digital commons.[36]

Benkler's proposal for a nonmarket, commons-based mode of production was undermined by the attention economy—as Benkler's own trajectory from the study of the digital commons to networked forms of propaganda also somehow indicates. Most p2p commons-based initiatives which were based on voluntary labor turned out to be unable to outcompete companies which were sustained and supported by the willingness of venture capitalists and financial markets to sustain prolonged losses with the expectations of the massive rewards that harnessing network effects through new kinds of quasi-monopolies entailed. The model of peers exchanging information and cooperating to produce common goods was overwhelmed by social media modes of communication. Clashes over values demonstrated the irreducibility of beliefs and desires to individual motivations and methodological individualism could not bear the weight of the history of oppression that sociogenically constructed subjects along differential axes of gender, sexuality, class, ethnicity and race.

Platformization, on the other hand, successfully turned the explosion of *participation* in digital communication into a growth in *revenue*. The growth of internet usage (from 361 million in the year 2000 to almost 2 billion in 2010, rising to over 5 billion in 2021) has thus been translated into the growth of market value of companies such as Google, Amazon, Facebook, Apple and Microsoft (whose aggregate market value in 2021 was estimated at 4 trillion US dollars).[37] This conversion of growth from participation to revenue is artfully captured by Benjamin Grosser's video *Order of Magnitude* (2019), whose supercut edits together sections of Facebook's CEO Mark Zuckenberg's public video appearances, emphasizing the compulsive frequency of terms such as "more," "grow," and metrics such as "millions" or "billions." The digital commons have thus been mostly expropriated or literally degraded—as described by Donatella Della Ratta's account of her experience as an advocate for Creative Commons in the Arab world at the turn of the 2010s. There she witnessed the enthusiasm for the creative commons in the region turn sour, as the relentless production of filmed evidence of police and military repression of dissent was first capitalized by a platform such as YouTube and then made to lose its status of evidence-image as networked propaganda took over what was once the internet.[38]

The tendency of capital to expropriate the commons—a process which inaugurated the birth of capitalism and has been carried out throughout its history—is, on the other hand, at the core of the theory of the Common such as articulated by the post-workerist Marxism I was engaging with throughout the 2010s. While the deployment of some version of institutional analysis in the theorization of networked commons-based modes of production relied mostly on the idea that the latter was going to outcompete the market, the notion of the Common deployed by post-workerist Marxism instead emphasized how the latter was just a new phase in a history of class struggle that was as old as the capitalist economy and indeed its very engine of development.

Post-workerist Marxists' concept of the Common departed from the centrality of methodological individualism and the nonrival nature of information as a good, because it did not start from the history and nature of property, but from the history and composition of labor. It did not start then from exchange in the market, but from production itself, that is, from social cooperation such as it takes place not only in the factory, but also throughout society. It argued that social cooperation as the source of the production of value in capitalist economies was no longer exclusively defined by the division of labor in the factory geared towards the production of material goods, but was increasingly geared towards that of information, knowledge, affects and relationality itself. It suggested that this shift entailed that capitalism increasingly functioned through a renewed expropriation of the Common, that is "the earth and all the resources associated with it: the land, the forests, the water, the air, minerals," but also "the results of human labor and creativity, such as ideas, language, affects, and so forth."[39] It posited that financialization corresponded to the dominant form of capital at the moment when the expropriation of the Common became the main modality of accumulation and indicated the growth of the percentage of rent (with relation to wages and profit) in the overall distribution of revenue as a symptom of this process. The hegemony of financial capital, which could be empirically verified by the new centrality of rent over wage and profit, signaled that the new strategy of accumulation of wealth had changed: unlike exploitation such as entailed by the wage-profit couplet, the centrality of rent in financial capital implied that "corporations steal the Common and transform it into property."[40] Thus the logic of financial capital from the point of view of value had become "extractivism"—a term that Sandro Mezzadra and Brett Neilson saw as including both data and mineral.[41] Foregrounding extractivism opens the Common to the critiques of Marxist political economy such as articulated from the perspective of political ecology, the Black radical tradition's rethinking of the law of value, and feminist foregrounding of social reproduction.[42] The necessary incomplete interaction between such perspectives does not easily fit into the neo-Promethean, accelerationist social project.

In this context, the notion that digital networks can become "infrastructures for the common" needs to question the very tenability and centrality of the network topos as well as dominant thinking about digital interfaces. Neither the industrial model of the factory nor the network imagery can account for or contain the forms of social cooperation in digital spaces. Capitalist digital social networks capture free labor by implementing a technosocial architecture whereby each node becomes a monad. Neomonadology is the diagram of the *dispositif* that captures and valorizes the free labor of technosocial cooperation. Here the distinction between lines and points, edges and vertices fades in the light of the relation between the quasi-infinite variations which make up the bulk of content and information shared and circulated, the patterning of communication by the forces of sympathy and antipathy, the affective flow of desires and beliefs, and the reconfiguration of the subject as point of view on such variations—not so much a rational individual, but some kind of neo-baroque darkly mirrored psychic interiority that keeps being affected by and folding in the outside.

Digital technologies are ever more embedded in natural, social and economic milieus in ways that call for new ways of inhabiting the world. The proliferation of echo chambers might not just be a feature of technosocial digital architectures but a reaction against the pressure of felt entanglement or differences-without-separability in the absence of new forms of technosocial reason where the computational innervates the social in a new way. Likes and dislikes, beliefs and disbeliefs, unthought motivations are the new psychic forces subtending modes of cooperation that do not imply division of labor but relations, such as following and being followed, shaped by the action of forces such as sympathy and antipathy, asymmetrical and mutual possession. The distinction between use values and exchange values that was basic to early Marxist political economy also becomes untenable as ethical, existential, and aesthetic values become the new ground of valorization. Under the pressure of entropic technosocial data embedding all kinds of values, the dream of master algorithms might turn out to generate unpredicted forms of fugitive alien intelligence. All of this, and much more, will surely come to affect the direction which the next decade, with its already heavy burden and threat of pandemic events, environmental catastrophes and global wars, might take.

— Naples, Italy, March 2022

1

New Economy, Financialization and
Social Production in the Web 2.0
(2009)

The internet and financial capital met for the first time in the mid-1990s—and it seemed, at least for a while, like a match made in heaven. On one side, an abundance of capital generated by the increasing availability of liquidity. On the other, a young and vibrant sector with the potential to establish dominance in potentially enormous new markets. The short years from the mid-1990s to the financial crash of the Nasdaq market of 2001 were a time when capital investment in the so-called digital economy enabled the formation of new labor cultures practiced by a multitude of micro-businesses that call themselves "dot-com." In this gold-rush atmosphere, generations of mostly young white males were literally invested with enormous flows of capital in a kind of generalized gamble that flooded with cash companies that mostly sold products and services online without requiring evidence of immediate profitability.[1]

The labor cultures that characterized this first wave of internet businesses looked very different from older corporate ones. Still riding the wave of the countercultural movements that participated in the invention of the personal computer, such as the Homebrew Computer Club, the new internet industry set itself up *against* the model of corporate computer labor *à la* IBM (suit and tie, the corporation hymn sung collectively in the morning, the company as a large, patriarchal corporate family).[2] Young entrepreneurs and dot-com workers used financial capital to finance ludic cultures. The classic gendered division of labor *à la Mad Men* (with men responsible for the most part for programming and women responsible for design and social relations) still persisted in an informal atmosphere that prolonged the soft heterosexuality of university life (think of Douglas Coupland's novels, especially *JPod*).[3] While the workplace atmosphere became playful and informal, new divisions, however, started to crystallize. For a select few, the wage as fixed income was quietly being integrated behind closed doors with shares in income generated by stock market options, while others were left behind.

As the pace of digital work has become as intense as a shoot'em up video game, relations of power have mutated from formal hierarchies into perverse interpersonal relations enacting the same dynamics as were masterfully displayed in the traumatic and theatrical unmasking of the true "boss" in Lars Von Trier's 2006 film *Direktøren for det hele* (*The Boss of it All*). At the same time, the wages of most new media workers are dropping to levels that are by far inferior to wages in the more traditional media.[4] Under the pressure of financialization, a schizophrenic working culture has emerged which, as Andrew Ross remarks, has absorbed the refusal of work of previous generations and transformed it into a new way of working, partially acknowledging the need for more freedom and informality arising out of a previous cycle of struggles, importing from academic labor the partial dissolution of the boundaries between work and leisure, and instigating in many cases a form of entrepreneurship that combines self-education and self-exploitation.[5]

With the 2001 stock market crash affecting technology shares sold in the Nasdaq market place, the so-called "dot-com bubble" clamorously popped, and for a moment it seemed as if the New Economy—which dreams of diffuse financial liquidity able to sustain new ways of working and producing—had suddenly and brutally been switched off in favour of a return to a war economy, in a new security version catalyzed by the terrorist attacks of 9/11. Was this the scrapping of the general intellect, as Franco Berardi affirmed at the time, in favor of a return to a war economy, with its new police and security inflection, as catalyzed by September 11?[6] The 2001 crash, however, did not so much end the digital economy as recalibrate it. Financial capital has reinvested in the internet, but on new bases. Already in 2004, Silicon Valley organic intellectuals such as Tim O'Reilly interpreted the crash as a signal that it was time to reorganize business on the internet. In order to do so, he pointed to the companies that survived the crash (Google and Amazon) as new models able to rebuild a "*new new economy*" out of the dot-com ruins.[7] According to O' Reilly, it was no longer enough to simply remediate models imported from the old economy, but one must learn from those companies that not only survived the crash, but also bucked the trend and thrived. The watchword of the new post-crash digital economy has thus become the "social web" or "Web 2.0."

Successful Web 2.0 companies, as O'Reilly argued, had some things in common: they used "the web as platform," and "data"; "harness[ed] collective intelligence," did not release software according to "the old cycle of updates," used "lightweight programming models," and implemented software that can be used by different devices. The Web 2.0 included companies that will later be called social media (Friendster, Facebook, Flickr, Myspace, Second Life, and Blogger), but also applications such as Google, inasmuch as the latter is built on the successful capacity of its algorithms to harness and extract value out of the browsing practices of its users. This model, O'Reilly argued, could be applied to other businesses that found ways to harness the value generated by common actions such as linking to or bookmarking websites, posting on a blog, commenting, modifying software and so on. Even Amazon, which at first sight in the early 2000s might have seemed like a simple remediation of a bookshop, survived the dot-com crash because, according to O'Reilly, it deploys a Web 2.0 model. It did not simply sell books, but it published user reviews on books using algorithms which fed on previous purchases and user profiles to "suggest" possible books to buyers.

This model, which survived the financial crash of 2001 and become the one to imitate, entailed the combination of new post-desktop software infrastructure, the active use of data, and especially the capacity to harness "collective intelligence," that is, users' social, affective and technological labor. The new frontier of the capitalist innovations of the new economy thus demand a new technical composition of labor, which reduces the amount of capital extracted out of waged work, increasing instead that of the "free labor" of users which it actively instigates and organizes.[8] The lesson was that capital had to invest in companies that demonstrably succeed in generating surplus value out of participation, that is, social life.[9]

The first decade of the 21st century, then, has been a crucial one in shaping new assemblages of value extraction. In many cases, surplus value has been derived through savings in the cost of labor that can be outsourced to users (as in "community" managers and users as beta-testers and producers of content) in exchange for free access.[10] The fundamental problem (and the fundamental resource) of the social web thus remains social cooperation, differentiated according to degrees of sociality and activity, starting with the "lowest" level constituted by the simple cumulative action of clicking a site or searching for multimedia materials up to a "higher" level such as open-source software production.[11] The post-crash wave of financialization has heavily invested in companies that can succesfully harness and monetize mass participation by users, that is, what Marxists would call a form of "social cooperation."

Financialization and the Fault of the Internet

In the 2000s, however, the foregrounding of users' participation turned out to be not simply a resource for a new breed of aggressive internet companies who could attract potential financial investors scared away by the dot-com crash, but also a threat to financial capital itself. By 2008, as the internet economy recovers from its first recession, a new, much larger and systemic financial crisis has invested the economy at large—wrecking lives and causing a real crisis of legitimacy for the capitalist economy. Starting with the so-called subprime market, the crisis has wiped out billions of dollars. For some, it is the internet's fault—and more specifically the fault of the new social internet (or Web 2.0).

In October 2008, a *Newsweek* editorial signed by Paul Kedrosky and entitled "The First Disaster of the Internet Age" turned the spotlight on Web 2.0, accusing it of being responsible for the catastrophe.[12] The editorial explicitly attacks the president of the US Federal Reserve, Alan Greenspan, who, before the dot-com financial crisis of 2001, maintained that the internet had positively transformed finance, making a "reallocation of risk" possible through the "creation, valuation and exchange of complex financial products on a global base."[13] Kedrosky reproaches Greenspan for not having foreseen how the decomposition and recomposition of financial products (such as the famous subprimes) could create problems for the valuation of titles, triggering a search for cash that went beyond any rational valuation and ignited the fuse of the future credit crisis. For Kedrosky, while it is true that the internet lowers transaction costs, it also contaminates financial capital by means of a new type of sociality, that of Web 2.0, which produces closed echo chambers of like-minded individuals.[14] It is within these echo chambers that the *Newsweek* editorial identifies the spaces of aggregation of "builders of exotic new products for the now $668 trillion [not a misprint] derivatives market."[15]

Instead of rendering markets more democratic and transparent, the internet is accused of generating a "fog of data" that helped Wall Street wiseguys derail the global economy as easily as if they were playing a video game. If the dot-com financial crisis is, overall, an adolescent internet crisis, 2008 is, for Kedrosky, "the first financial crisis of the mature internet age—a crisis caused in large part by the tightly coupled technologies that now undergird the financial system and our society as a whole."[16] Internet traders are thus said to lack that intrinsic rationality that permits the market to correctly assess commercial value. The ease with which the internet allows for the buying and selling of shares exponentially multiplies the number of transactions that become practically untraceable in ways that increase market volatility.

As sociologist of finance Karin Knorr Cetina points out, interaction with the screen had already changed financial markets, long before the internet enabled mass financial trading, making the former fundamentally different from older market models such as anthropological ones based on gifts and those founded on the production of goods for consumer markets.[17] As financial markets become "fully visible on the screen—as a whole of pieces subjected to rapid, interchangeable, altogether contextualized changes," for Knorr Cetina, they become actionable "through a complex series of financial tools." As a result, she argues, financial markets entail a "global intersubjectivity that comes from the characteristics of these markets as reflexively observed by the participants on their computer screens in an immediacy, synchronicity and temporal continuity."[18]

According to Kedrosky, once explicitly hooked onto the internet, this global inter-subjectivity driven by computer screens has generated a "shadow-banking system" that, in 2007, is as big as the traditional one. This is an economy that can no longer be separated from the social web culture, subjected to the power of influencers, deploying instant messaging to close financial transactions. For *Newsweek*, the internet also allows for the proliferation of financial "inventions," such as derivatives, which are treated as "a cross between gossip and video games [...]. Trivial conversations over instant messaging can mutate into trades. Everything is flattened, with chatter about the weather right alongside setting up a $100 million default swap. What matters when everything looks the same and is bookended with a happy face?"[19]

Kedrosky concludes by arguing for a better technological solution to minimize social interaction amongst financial operators: a new web-based interface, such as an electronic dashboard with quadrants and a color-coded system (curiously similar to the alert system created by the Bush administration to warn the population about the risks of terrorist attacks) that could facilitate the self-evaluation of financial markets.[20] In short, what is proposed is a new web protocol for finance capable of subtracting the rational economic agent from the irrational imitative sociality of the network.

The proposal to create a "financial dashboard" for the web is an example of the drive to discipline mass financial transactions, making them transparent through a new technological mediation and defusing the dangerous convergence between the social web of bloggers, Facebook, MSN and Myspace with finance. The financial market 2.0 is a market that, in newspapers and television reports, is ever more vulnerable to social emotions such as fear, anxiety and panic. It is a market that produces herd reactions to the signals from economic indexes, political statements and consumer behaviors. Inasmuch as the "sense" of the market is seen as constructed at the level of the formation of public opinion, the techno-solution involves distancing the operator and the market as a social assemblage by means of data analytics which can reconstruct a more objective and intelligible aggregated meaning out of numerous market signals, that is, its perceptions, sensations and affects.

This intelligible sense of the market is the ideal aspiration of econometric models and simulations, which represent something like the opposite of the susceptible social affectability of the Web 2.0 financial trader. In the 2000s, financial objectivity is the domain of so-called "risk managers," a specialized group of financial operators with technical skills which warrant higher pay than simple operators. This new breed of financial specialists are often mathematicians and physicists from the ex-Soviet Bloc and India, who can apply to the financial market the statistical models and stochastic simulations used in their former disciplines.[21] Amongst the most famous of such models, one can find for example the Black-Scholes method for representing the course of financial products over time, or the Monte Carlo, which Nassim Nicholas Taleb, a Lebanese professor of the "science of uncertainty" at the University of Massachusetts (Amherst) and discretely successful "risk manager" on Wall Street, describes in his editorial success *Fooled by Randomness: The Hidden Role of Chance in Life and in the Markets* (2004).[22] The Monte Carlo model, originally developed by physicists at Los Alamos to study the chain reactions of the atom, is commonly used to simulate a whole series of scenarios over time, determining a series of "evolutive paths" within a "phase-space" that can establish the possible variations of highly volatile market prices.[23]

Inspired by the work of the economist Robert Shiller, author of *Irrational Exuberance* (2000), and famous for having questioned the "efficient market model"[24] already in the early '80s, Taleb relates price trends, that is, the way in which the various scenarios dealing with price trends can vary according to the Monte Carlo simulation, not only to statistical and physical factors, but also to the behaviors, conducts and even physiological reactions of stock market operators. What these models aim to simulate is the behavior of an assemblage, such as that of financial markets, that encompasses a multitude of variables and cultures which in the 2000s are comprised of the social web and MSN instantaneous messaging cultures, mathematical and physical cultures dedicated to financial advising, and even the culture of financial operators in global cities such as London, New York and Tokyo.[25] The physiology of financial markets thus comprises the pharmacopornographic hormonal surplus value of testosterone which according to a study by the Department of Physiology Development in Neuroscience of the University of Cambridge increases the possibility of making successful investments, making them literally testosterone junkies.[26]

Networks Vs. Network and Ethico-Artistic Experimentation

From the point of view of new technologies, therefore, financial capital works like a network of networks composed not just of individual nodes but also of technical, cultural, social and physiological components. At the same time, however, as theorists of cognitive and affective labor point out, given that workers in the capitalist mode of production do not produce value individually, but always by engaging in social cooperation, labor also increasingly operates as a network and through networks. From a Marxist perspective, according to which capital is a conflictual social relation between classes, class struggle can also be seen as a question of networks against networks. At the turn of the 21st century, the question of the war *between* networks was actually the object of numerous studies, both by groups close to the American military establishment and from the point of view of the elaboration of new forms of political struggles.[27] Recently, for example, Eugene Thacker and Alexander R. Galloway have proposed a new political tactic which they refer to as the "exploit."[28] They call *protocological struggles* the modality of conflict which involves networks against networks, thus foregrounding the importance of technical protocols in the governance of networked spaces. They argue that political resistance in both technological and vital/biological networks implies the discovery of weaknesses or holes in existent technologies as its fundamental modality. The political practices implied in the struggles between networks or assemblages are for them characterized by a lack of distinction between organic and inorganic, technological and biological levels and imply the identification of leaks or holes in the very composition of networks and their immanent modalities of control. "The scope of political resistance in vital networks, then, should be the discovery of these exploits—or better yet: look for traces of exploits and you will find political practices."[29] Such political practices, however, are not grasped as simple acts of resistance, but involve the projection of potential mutations through the opening glimpsed and utilized by the *exploit*.[30] They do not declare traditional forms of struggle obsolete, but assert the necessity of introducing a new strategic level of struggle, one which is constituted by specific forms of control entailing intrinsic weaknesses that can be found in large biological and technological assemblages organized as networks.

Such an approach is currently explicitly practiced by artists, as in the two ethical artistic experimentations which I will describe below. These experiments address financial networks through the tactic of the exploit with a view of provoking catastrophic events targeted specifically at financial capital. The first involves a group of activists known as The Yes Men (a collective name attributed to the Americans Andy Bichlbaum and Mike Bonanno and their admirers/imitators), while the second bears the name GWEI (Google Will Eat Itself) an artistic project by Ubermorgen.com, Alessandro Ludovico and Paolo Cirio.

The Yes Men, a well-known group of cultural activists, experiment with actions targeting the network of corporate and governmental public relations agents. Taking advantage of the systemic chaos induced by the multiplicity of communicative sources active in networks (what *Newsweek* called "the fog of data"), and starting with the assumption that the practice of public relations consists in masking the brutally cynical ideological assumptions of corporations and governmental organizations, The Yes Men create websites, for example, that perfectly imitate those of the targeted organization, and accept invitations sent to the site to participate in events, conferences and interviews under the guise of the organizations that they pretend to be.[31] Assuming the authoritative aura of official representatives (they have impersonated spokespeople from the World Trade Organization, McDonald's, Halliburton, Exxon, Dow Chemical and even the Department of Housing and Urban Development of the US government, for example), they make proposals that, although shocking for many, they believe correspond to the fundamental underlying ethos of these organizations. For example, they have proposed to audiences of investors and lobbyists to legalize the sale of votes and even to make the poor eat recycled human excrement. It seems that the majority of their proposals are received in a relatively favorable way, or at least without indignation or shock by their listeners. The Yes Men then proceed to publish and disseminate to the general public their proposals as well as the reactions of the investors and lobbyists.

In 2004, one of the Yes Men was invited on air by the BBC and publicly announced that Dow Chemical would compensate the victims of the Bhopal disaster, paying $12 billion to survivors. This false announcement, even if unmasked in a timely fashion by Dow Chemical, caused a 3.4% drop in Dow stocks on the Frankfurt market and a fifty-cent drop on the New York market.[32] In the "fog of data" and in the proliferation of communication sources condemned by Kedrosky, The Yes Men identify a weak point in the assemblage of public relations that plays an important role in establishing, for example, the value of stock prices on financial markets. With carefully planned actions, their intent is not so much to cause micro-shocks that in the end are easily handled by the corporations under attack, as much as to show the vulnerability of the assemblages that establish the value of financial titles to these types of actions.

Another example of ethical and artistic experimentation with protocol struggle practices is at work in the Google Will Eat Itself project (GWEI), an Italo-Austrian collaboration between Ubermorgen.com, Alessandro Ludovico and Paolo Cirio. Launched in 2005, GWEI works in a very simple way. It identifies the fundamental source of income for the corporation in Google's "Adsense" program, which connects hundreds of thousands of small advertisements to websites globally. The two artists opened a large number of Adsense accounts and hid them in a series of websites. Every time someone visits one of these sites, a mechanism is activated that assigns to the overall network of sites a monthly micropayment from Google. Once the necessary amount to buy an actual share of Google is reached, the authors use it to purchase the former thus turning the project into a means to use Google to buy Google.

The provocation launched by this act of computer cannibalism has been framed as an act of criticism of Google's economic model and what the authors consider its fake benevolence ("do no evil"). In "Hack the Google self.referentialism" (the theoretical text that explains the project's assumptions),[33] the artists accuse Google of being a dictator exercising its power through a new type of monopoly in a number of strategic sectors of the internet economy. Google's database, in particular, already appears as a enormous privatized resource. Users are depicted as being oblivious to this ongoing process of data accumulation, held in a hypnotic state by an almost perfect machine, accepting AdSense as a means to monetize their activities but also contributing to the consolidation of these new gigantic monopolies:

> They accept to display this tiny text advertisment [sic] in exchange of a small amount of money for every click on them. This process is protected and monitored to prevent abuse. The final (actual) scenario is Google as the giant middleman. It sucks money from the advertisers offering a targeted portion of the global webspace. And it gives spare change to the publishers for their collaboration. It sucks info from the websites (and news, images, prices) and it releases it to the user's

queries. Being in the middle it is more and more the unavoidable balancing center of the system. But we're not talking about a natural system. We're talking about business and pre-dominance.[34]

The GWEI authors conclude by highlighting this loophole, the leak or exploit, as Thacker and Galloway would call it, through which it seems possible to pick at the benevolent dictatorship of Google and others. "The greatest enemy of such a giant is not another giant: it's the parasite. If enough parasitites [sic] suck small amounts of money [...], they will empty this artificial mountain of data and its inner risk of digital totalitarianism."[35]

Can these small loopholes, as spotted and exploited by the *Yes Men* and *Ubermorgen* really jam the financial capital machine and its perverse mechanisms? This is not the right question to ask of these ethical-artistic experiments. They seem to have an essentially heuristic value, in the sense indicated by Galloway and Thacker. The process of finding and setting into motion an exploit opens up an experimentation that touches a wide range of concatenations in neoliberal societies struck by the effects of an economic governmentality that intensifies levels of exploitation, mortifies life, ravages social relations and impoverishes subjec-tivity. On the other hand, there is no possible reform of financial markets, simply the overcoming of financial capitalism and its hold on contemporary societies.

2

Attention, Economy and the Brain

(2012)

> *"Whoever treats of interest inevitably treats of attention [...]"*
> — William James

> *"I consume my consumers."*
> —Grace Jones, "Corporate Cannibal"

> *"Attention, conatus of the brain [...]"*
> — Gabriel Tarde

In the early 21st century, the notion of attention has come to occupy a key place within the overall discourse surrounding what has been called "the new economy" or "digital economy," but also within the critical analyses of cultural theorists evaluating the politics of digital media. Theories of the attention economy are a continuation of the modern theme of the "crisis of attentiveness," this time elaborated in terms of the impact of internet usage on the cognitive architecture of a neuroplastic and mimetic social brain.[1] The notion of "attention" is mobilized as an economic category within theories of the internet, framed in terms of neoclassical or mainstream economics theory *and* within theories attempting to account for processes of psychic transindividuation and social cooperation in contemporary capitalism.

The prominence of the notion of attention to theorizations of the economy of the internet and digital media at the turn of the 2010s marks a significant difference with regard to the centrality of information in earlier theorizations of this kind.[2] While information was said to be a radically new type of commodity that challenged established economic models, attention seems to bring with it a re-coding of the economy of new media along more orthodox lines, inasmuch as it reintroduces a principle of scarcity where there used to be only abundance and limitless possibilities. If information is bountiful, attention is scarce because it indicates the limits inherent to the neurophysiology of perception and the social limitations to time available for consumption.

In an earlier phase, new media economists stressed the abundance of information in the digital economy as part of a new inflection of economic Darwinism, where the survival of the fittest was not as important as the capacities of a proliferating, connected life to create the new. This was an artificial kind of life, which the digital entrepreneur had to learn to harness and selectively channel in order to extract surplus value.[3] The *bios* of the new economy, then, entailed a continuity with the Darwinian dynamics of competition, while eschewing the harsh constraints of natural scarcity which framed the notion of the survival of the fittest. The return of scarcity in theories of the attention economy imply a normalization of the digital economy. However, the latter manifests a tension between the previous, abundant, inventive *bios* of organic life and the new centrality accorded to the *bios* of a special organ, the brain, but one that is strangely deprived of its capacity for creation and innovation.

In theories of the attention economy, attention is first of all a scarce resource, which is what allows the internet to become an economic medium again, that is, a medium to which all the axioms of market economics can once again be applied. Scarcity is the condition that can give rise to a proper economy, the "attention economy." Attention is a scarce resource because "the sum total of human attention is necessarily limited and therefore scarce."[4] For Michael Goldhaber, for example, the notion of the "attention economy" indicates "a system that revolves primarily around paying, receiving, and seeking what is most intrinsically limited and not replaceable by anything else, namely the attention of other human beings."[5]

According to theorists of the attention economy, inasmuch as attention is both scarce and measurable, it can become not simply a commodity like others, but a kind of capital. The abstract quality of attention and at the same time the fact that the "attentional assemblages" of digital media enable automated forms of measurement (as in "clicks," "downloads," "likes," "views," "followers," and "sharings" of digital objects) open it up to marketization and financialization (from the floating value of internet companies to the accumulation of celebrity capital by means of a number of followers on Twitter to the changing value of "clicks" as calculated by Google"s software AdSense and AdWords).[6] A whole new data processing and mining industry is thus born on the back of social quantities harvested which literally reflect the social distribution and intensity of attention.

Although Georg Franck had already attempted to describe attention as "the new currency of business" in 2009, proposing that attention constituted a new kind of capital ("attentive capital") and even a kind of wage or income (attention income such as that generated by fame and celebrity, for example), the attempts to capitalize attention in the early 2000s went even further.[7] Thus, for example, the Wikipedia entry for "attention economy" reported proposals for "attention transactions" (Goldhaber); the institution of new property rights in attention; and, of course, also the issuing of "attention bonds," that is, "small warranties that some information will not be a waste of the recipient's time, placed into escrow at the time of sending."[8] One such proposed scheme, for example, suggested that "receivers could cash in their bonds to signal to the sender that a given communication was a waste of their time or elect not to cash them in to signal that more communication would be welcome."[9]

It is true that such theories constituted a kind of "fringe" discourse within the field of economics at large, and one that lacked the legitimacy that is usually granted to more academic work. Published mostly on the internet, and then also occasionally translated into paperback publications for the market of incumbent and aspiring internet entrepreneurs, they constituted a specific genre which, while also being somehow ephemeral, in some way translated the more general preoccupations of economic actors operating within the context of what used to be called the "new economy." In particular, as Henry Jenkins argued in his study of "convergence culture," the notion of attention as a scarce resource corresponded to the preoccupations of corporate giants when facing a new context of communication characterized both by a large offer of information and a new type of consumer/viewer who was tendentially in a state of drift.[10]

Digitization and networking, and the special status of information as a non-rival good, here do not produce the conditions for the emergence of a new "nonmarket" mode of production, but rather point to the circularity of normative market economics. By consuming attention and making it scarce, the wealth of information creates poverty that in its turn produces the conditions for a new market to emerge. This new market requires specific techniques of maximization of attention, specific techniques of evaluation (algorithms, data analytics) and units of measurement (clicks, likes, shares, viewings, followers, friends, impressions, tags, etc.).

A Poverty of Attention

Within current discussions of the economic implications of shifts in technologies of attention, the latter is seen not only as "scarce" because limited, but also as increasingly "degraded." In a strange reversal of early information theory's take on entropy, attention here becomes the quantity which is "consumed" by that which is abundant, that is, information. In the wave of publishing around the idea of a "crisis of attention" (which parallels and supplements discussions of attention economy), it is thus common to find the notion of a "degradation of attention" provoked by digital technologies and its economic effects. In an article by Sam Anderson in *New York Magazine* on May 25, 2009, one finds, for example, a quote referring back to the writings of "polymath economist" Herbert A. Simon, who in 1971 offered what Anderson describes as "maybe the most concise possible description of our modern struggle." For Anderson, information literally "consumes the attention of its recipients." As Simon put it, "a wealth of information creates a poverty of attention, and a need to allocate that attention efficiently among the overabundance of information sources that might consume it." For Anderson, "[a]s beneficiaries of the greatest information boom in the history of the world, we are suffering, by Simon's logic, a correspondingly serious poverty of attention."[11]

If attention that is actually paid can be measured by numbers of clicks and viewings, however, attention that is lost in paying attention requires a different kind of measurement. If the financialization of attention relies on the possibility of measuring attention by means of techniques operating on data and meta-data abstracted from digital interaction, the poverty of attention is related to the measurement of physiological reactions of the brain to stimuli and to the new neuroplastic potential of the brain. As Anderson explains,

> Before the sixties, they measured it through easy-to-monitor senses like vision and hearing (if you listen to one voice in your right ear and another in your left, how much information can you absorb from either side?), then eventually graduated to PET scans and EEGs and electrodes and monkey brains. Only in the last ten years—thanks to neuroscientists and their functional MRIs—have we been able to watch the attending human brain in action, with its coordinated storms of neural firing, rapid blood surges, and oxygen flows. This has yielded all kinds of fascinating insight [...][12]

In a widely read essay published in 2009 in *Wired* magazine and later turned into a book, Nicholas Carr weaves together such research to formulate an argument that resonates with interest on the part of digital media economists in the value of attention.[13] Citing research by neuroscientists on experimental exposure to new media objects, Carr argues that such exposure rewires neural pathways within individual brains. Digital media re-wires the brain, as activities such as multitasking and reading hyperlinked texts would produce, both in seasoned internet users and new ones, a shift of neuronal activity from the hippocampus (where brain scientists usually locate activities such as focused reasoning and long term memory) to the prefrontal cortex (which would be occupied by rote tasks and short term memory). Exposure to digital media is thus said to remodel different types of memory within individual brains, making individuals faster at carrying out routine tasks, but at the same time less efficient in the ways they carry out those tasks and weaker at deeper comprehension and understanding.[14]

In neuroscience, these ambivalent properties of the brain's attentive capacities are understood through the notion of *plasticity*, which Catherine Malabou in her controversial essay on neuroscience and the spirit of capitalism calls "the dominant concept of the neurosciences [...] their common point of interest, their dominant motif and their privileged operating model."[15] The brain for Carr has been rewired by the Web in such a way as to make it a faster automaton when it comes to routine tasks but at the price of severely impairing its "higher" cognitive faculties. The economic/informational plastic brain is thus caught in a double bind: on the one hand, in order to participate in the attention economy, it must enter a technological assemblage of attention; on the other hand, becoming part of this assemblage implies a dramatic cognitive loss that is translated into a subjectivity more adept at carrying out routine tasks but less capable of reasoning, reflecting and intimacy.[16]

The "brain scientists" quoted by Carr had already described the attentional assemblage of brain and internet as a *costly* one for the efficiency of thinking:

> The Internet is an interruption system. It seizes our attention only to scramble it. [...] The penalty is amplified by what brain scientists call switching costs. Every time we shift our attention, the brain has to reorient itself, further taxing our mental resources. Many studies have shown that switching between just two tasks can add substantially to our cognitive load, impeding our thinking and increasing the likelihood that we'll overlook or misinterpret important information. On the Internet, where we generally juggle several tasks, the switching costs pile ever higher.[17]

In this sense, the attention economy brings to the fore and makes explicit the long tendency of modern culture to produce what Jonathan Crary has called an "ongoing crisis of attentiveness" in which "the changing configurations of capitalism continually push attention and distraction to new limits and thresholds, with an endless sequence of new products, sources of stimulation, and streams of information, and then respond with new methods for managing and regulating perception."[18] For Crary, in fact, the crisis of attentiveness goes back to the nineteenth century, where already the notion of attention within the new assemblages of production and consumption of industrial capitalism provided the means by which a new type of subject was constituted. This was the beginning of what he also calls "a revolutionizing of the means of perception," which for the last hundred years has exposed perceptual modalities to "a state of perpetual transformation, or, some might claim, a state of crisis."[19] As Crary also argues, however, already in its early days, "the articulation of a subject in terms of attentive capacities simultaneously disclosed a subject incapable of conforming to such disciplinary imperatives."[20]

When read together, both statements about the attention economy and the crisis of attention point to the reconfiguration of the attentive capacities of the subject in ways which constitute attention at the same time as a *scarce*, and hence a *valuable resource*, while also producing an *impoverished subject*. The brain provides the scarce resource that allows the digital economy to be normalized, while also suffering a depletion of its cognitive capacities. This seems akin to what Bernard Stiegler calls the "*proletarianization of the life of the mind*," which remains one of the possible outcomes of the diffusion of digital and reticulated technologies.[21]

Paying Attention and Imitation

The economic subject of attention as it is drawn by theories of the attention economy also expresses another challenge, this time produced not only by individual exposure to new media technologies, but also by the technosociality of the connected brain. It is neither, then, only a matter of what the individual does when accumulating or spending their limited stock of attention nor simply a question of the degradation of the individual's capacity to pay attention as the cost incurred by being constantly plugged into the attentional assemblages of digital media. Paying attention to what others do on networked social platforms triggers potential processes of imitation by means of which network culture produces and reproduces itself. The brain mobilized by theories of the attention economy in a milieu of reticulated communication is measurably social.[22]

Participating in the attentional assemblages of digital media implies becoming part of technosocial processes where paying attention triggers responses of imitation which shift between the virtual form of a passing impression and the actual form of acts such as reading and writing, watching and listening, copying and pasting, downloading and uploading, liking, sharing, following and bookmarking. The economy of attention is, then, also the economy of the socialization of ideas, affects and percepts, and hence an economy of automated technosocial production and cooperation. But are theories of the attention economy equipped to deal with the socially productive character of attentional assemblages or do they remain confined to an individual model of cognition which is too centered on the individual brain? How do they account for the ways in which thinking is becoming distributed between human and non-human agents?

As Charles T. Wolfe argues, at the turn of the 21st century, the neurosciences begin "to take something of a 'social' turn [...], with the publication of books, anthologies, and journal issues called *Social Neuroscience*, *Social Brain* and such, picking up momentum in the past five years. Topics such as imitation, empathy, 'mind-reading,' and even group cognition have come to the fore."[23] In particular the "social" in social cognition "focuses notably on mirror neurons, which indicate the existence in the brain of a particular recognition or decoding of *action* and thus of the imitation of action, implying an understanding of other people's intentions, goals and desires."[24] The notion of mirror neurons for Wolfe opens up discussion of the brain to new materialist accounts of the social intellect, but unfortunately at this stage it tends to rely on sociobiological theories of primate behavior and hence sees the "social intellect" as driven by a "Machiavellian intelligence."[25] This is a recoding of networked subjectivity onto the figure of the manipulative primate, whose social intelligence is imitative in nature and where imitation is basically the key to social manipulation by a self-interested, calculative subject endowed with "strategic rationality."[26] It is, then, a social intellect which is ultimately determined by the calculative, self-interested rationality of *homo oeconomicus*.[27]

What is at stake in the relation between attention and imitation evoked by theories of the attention economy is a new translation in economic terms of the theme of imitative, swarming and contagious behaviors as characterizing networked communication.[28] The neuroplastic brain, then, not only reconfigures its cognitive architecture in response to new media exposure, but, when seen together with the enactive and involuntary impressions produced by paying attention as an act of potential imitation, turns the self-possessive and rational economic subject into a potentially *mimetic node* within a logical network. And yet, processes of social emergence which characterize the discourse on innovation in theories of the information economy are here downplayed. In the wake of the financial crisis of 2008, theories of financial markets such as André Orléan's focused on the contagious and mimetic behaviors undermining the notion of the rationality of the economic agent, for example, short-circuiting rational choice through imitation.[29] Paying attention in a socially networked environment, then, exposes the paradox of a self-interested, calculative subject who is, however, at the same time also exposed to the forces of mimesis and contagion.

Attention, Value, Cooperation

In an early essay entitled "For a Redefinition of the Concept of 'Bio-politics,'" Maurizio Lazzarato asks us to reconsider the well-known post-workerist thesis that the information economy no longer captures and puts to work the "time of work," but rather the "time of life."[30] As Lazzarato argues, the concept of the "time of life" implied in the information economy evokes what he calls "an a-organic life" by which he means "time and its virtualities": "Not abstract time, measured time, but time as *puissance*, time as 'source of continuous creation of unpredictable novelties,' 'that which allows everything to be done,' according to some statements of Bergson."[31] For Lazzarato, the information economy mobilizes a new kind of vitalism "that is *temporal* and not just *organic*, a vitalism that refers to the virtual and not simply to biological processes."[32]

In the early 2000s, such a-organic life acquired an organic character that was evident in the increasing salience of neuroscience and its object, the brain. As we have seen, the cognitive architecture of the brain organized by principles of the neurophysiological limits to attention, the neuroplasticity of brain cells, and the imitative capacity of mirror neurons provides the organic reference that determines the way the brain acts as a force in theories of the attention economy and networked media. In his later work on Gabriel Tarde, however, Lazzarato also explicitly assumes the concept of "brain-memory" as a means to conceptualize the character of such a-organic life, as the basis of his critique of mainstream and Marxist political economy inasmuch as both of these theories, in his opinion, fail to account for the production of value as the result of social cooperation.

Lazzarato draws on Tarde's specific deployment of the brain as a model for his theory of social cooperation inasmuch as nerve cells exhibit peculiar features within the larger milieu of biological life. They are the most homogeneous and least specialized of the cells of the body, but most importantly, they are connected to each other in such a way as to influence each other's states even at a great distance. Synaptical connections enacted by axons defy the physical proximity of neurons, generating what Malabou calls the "general landscape of memory."[33] Furthermore Tarde's "brain-memory" is not an individual organ belonging to a subject, but it is by nature constituted by the outside, a fold crossed and shaped by the currents produced by the circulation of the social quanta of beliefs and desires. In Tarde's psychological economy, brain cells are open monads, infolding the outside and reactualizing it at every turn.[34]

In Tarde's account, communication technologies such as the press enable the socius to become more akin to the network of neural cells in the central nervous system. They imply a conception of subjectivity as that which unfolds in relation to action-at-a-distance by other subjectivities or monads, making our alliances and ideas more fluid and less set in tradition. Economic value, he argues, is derivative with relation to social, cultural and aesthetic values, which are the product of social cooperation or cooperation between brains, whose labor is defined as the "labor of attention." Attention, defined as the "conatus of the brain," is that which expresses the desire of the brain-memory to affect and be affected through this peculiar form of action at a distance. Memory (or spirit, or soul) expresses our power of acting on the world and its labor is above all the labor of attention.[35]

The labor of attention enables social cooperation and is thus the real source of the production of value—a *social* kind of production steeped in relationality. The openness of the brain-memory to action-at-a-distance by other brain-memories is what allows the value produced by invention to be socialized through imitation. It does not leave the economic subject exposed to the irrational capture by external forces, but it implies that it is sociality as such that realizes value.[36]

Psycho-powers

Tarde considers the invention of modern communication technologies as positive inasmuch as they increase such powers of cooperation and extend the reach of mutual influence modern media enhances, and extends the range and scope of those processes of invention and imitation that for him constitute the essence of economic life. In Bernard Stiegler's work, however, what he calls "attentional" or "psycho" technologies, such as radio, television and digital technologies, have done more than simply extend the powers of mutual affection of connected brains.[37] Starting from a reading of Edmund Husserl's phenomenology that is substantially at odds with Lazzarato's emphasis on "a-organic life" (and his overall philosophy of difference), Stiegler reads modern media as "tertiary retentions" or "mnemotechnic technologies" which concretize modes of "psycho-power" affecting the relation of self to self and self to other. Attention is the name for that relation between "retentions" and "protentions," that is, between the movement of consciousness that retains the trace of that which has just passed and its expectation of that which is to come. For Stiegler, in modern societies, the relation between retentions and protentions is mediated by those specific instances of tertiary retentions that are the media as psychotechnologies.

From this perspective, the contemporary economy of attention needs to be read as a new moment in the long duration of modern media as psycho and social technologies. Such media have historically enacted "the systematic capture of attention [...] resulting in a constant industrial canalization of attention," whose effects on libidinal energy have been substantially destructive. What they have destroyed is, on the one hand, a set of knowledges which he describes as "savoir-vivre" (which corresponds to the Foucauldian notion of "care of the self") and civility (care of others as founded on "philia," that is socialised libidinal energy), and, on the other, the "psychical apparatus and the social apparatus" as a whole.[38]

For Stiegler, it is not a question of denouncing the technical colonization of libidinal energy by technique (inasmuch as technique, as he argued in *Technics and Time* (1998), following André Leroi-Gourhan, is a constitutive element of anthropogenesis), but of considering the harmful effects of the industrial economy, based on the division between production and consumption, and on the quality of socialized libidinal energy.[39] If the attention economy somehow degrades the quality of libidinal energy, this is not due to some intrinsic limits of the human capacity to pay attention or to the inevitable effects of technique, but rather to a specific conception and organization of the economic system which overlooks the importance of libidinal energy to the production of the psyche and the social.[40] This conception and organization has caused the processes of individuation that connect psychic and social life to be short-circuited, resulting in the destructive hegemony of the short term over the long term. This is something equivalent to the new tragedy of the commons, brought about by corporate enclosure. For Stiegler, social network technologies, like those associated with social media, intervene exactly in this milieu of psychic proletarianization provoked by modern media and marketing techniques:

> It is a matter of technologies of indexation, annotation, tags and modelised traces (M-traces),

wiki technologies and collaborative technologies in general [...]. After having destroyed the traditional social networks, the psychotechnologies become social technologies, and they tend to become a new milieu and a new reticular condition of transindividuation grammatising new forms of social relations.[41]

It is important to underline that, for Stiegler, social network technologies were not necessarily bound to extend the psychic and social impoverishment that the marketing and consumption-driven modern media perpetrated. On the contrary, the new forms of social relations grammatised by social networks produce new conditions of transindividuation that might allow for a reversal of the hegemony of modern psychotechnologies. For him, paying attention to social networks could potentially imply truly taking care of self and others in ways that could renew depleted libidinal energy and trigger the emergence of a new collective organization.

Conclusion

Tracing the properties attributed to attention in theories of the attention economy we can see, then, how the former enacts a tense relation among a number of attributes of attention as a measurable economic entity: scarcity (as a limit that signals a return of "normal" economics within the "new" economy); poverty (the qualitative degradation of attention); and imitation (the vulnerability of the brain to capture by external forces quantified by the measurement of the diffusion of behaviors such as liking, following, etc). Attention is scarce from the point of view of the seller/provider of corporate commodities; it is poor when conceived from the point of view of efficient performance.[42] Theories of the attention economy, then, appear locked within the limits of scarcity, unable to account for the powers of invention of networked subjectivities, falling back into "herd-like" models of connected sociality, and delegating to speculative mechanisms of financialization the capacity to create value out of partial attention and continuous distraction.

On the other hand, for critics of political economy such as Stiegler and Lazzarato, the concept of attention is enrolled within a general framework aiming at overcoming the impoverishment and scarcity provoked by the subsumption of attention under capital (or, in the terms used in this article, the ways in which attention is used to "normalize" the excessive abundance of the information economy). In such a context, attention does not simply indicate the effort by which the individual brain works, nor can it be reduced to a scarce, and hence tradeable commodity, or to that which exposes the individual to a dramatic cognitive impoverishment. On the contrary, attention is the process by which value is produced as inseparable from the technological production of subjectivity such as formed within and by the Common. This involves a social logic of invention and diffusion of common desires, beliefs, and affects.

What I have mapped here, then, is a bifurcation in thinking about attention and the economy which exposes two very different ways of organizing a practice of paying attention. While theories of the attention economy, however, correspond to explicit commercial and business practices of organizing and managing attention, what we need is a further exploration of other ways in which paying attention can become a practice that will be able to produce different forms of subjectivity and different models of what an economy of social cooperation could be like.

3

Ordinary Psychopathologies of
Cognitive Capitalism

(2013)

> *"There is no life whatsoever without norms of life, and the morbid state is always a certain mode of living. "*
> — Georges Canguilhem

Capitalism is pathological, Deleuze and Guattari once said. Like all societies, it is rational and irrational at the same time. It is rational in its mechanisms, its cogs and wheels, its connecting systems and even in the place it assigns to the irrational. Logistical and productive arrangements, the organization of the factory floor or the office space, sophisticated cybernetic and telematic technologies, rules, regulations, protocols and markets, data analytics and engagement metrics, all is reasonable, yet only if one accepts its axioms. "It's like theology, everything about it is rational if you accept sin, immaculate conception, incarnation." Underneath, however, it is a different story: it is delirium, drift. "The stock market is certainly rational: one can understand it, study it, the capitalists know how to use it, and yet it is completely delirious, it's mad [...] the system is demented, yet it works very well at the same time."[1] What one should be looking at, Deleuze and Guattari argue, is the way in which each specific society distributes the relation between what is rational ("the interests being defined in the framework of this society, the way people pursue these interests, their realization") and what is irrational ("desires, investments of desire [...] on which interests depend in their determination and distribution of an enormous flux, all kind of libidinal-unconscious flows that make up the delirium of this society").[2] It is this distribution that underlies the distinction between the "normal" and the "pathological."

Is there a specific distribution of the rational and the irrational, of interests and desires, of the normal and the pathological in what a strand of Marxist theory defines as "cognitive capitalism"? Cognitive capitalism is just one of a number of terms that have tried to politically inflect the "colorless" notion of the knowledge or information economy. The insistence on the term "capitalism" stresses the invariance of the fundamentals of the capitalist mode of production, such as the "fundamental role played by profit and the centrality of the wage relation, or more precisely of the different forms of waged labor on which the extraction of surplus value depends."[3] As such it is part of a range of new terms that have also tried to question the uncritical identification of the economy with the capitalist economy *tout court* (such as communicative capitalism, semioinfocapitalism, biocapitalism, neoliberal capitalism, platform capitalism and the like).[4] Theories of cognitive capitalism in particular deploy the term "cognitive" to define "the new nature of work, the new sources of values and forms of property which provide the basis for the accumulation of capital [...]."[5] Carlo Vercellone, for example, claims that the term "cognitive" is employed to define the main source of value which now lies within "the knowledges and the creative capacities of living labor [...]. The importance of routine-based productive activities and material labor which consists in transforming material resources by mean of material tools and machines, decreases in favor of a new paradigm of work, simultaneously more intellectual, immaterial and relational."[6]

The theory of cognitive capitalism, then, specifically addresses the ways in which capitalism no longer simply exploits the capacity of the human body to perform manual, repetitive work in the assembly line but increasingly mobilizes its cognitive capacities. Inasmuch as knowledge production is by its nature not subject to the same kind of homogeneous measurement that grounds the law of value in industrial capitalism, it produces something that exceed and a tension in relation to industrial capitalist extraction of surplus value. In the terms provided by this theory, cognitive labor undermines the classical law of value, inasmuch as its productivity can no longer be measured through the arithmetic instrument of the working hour or confined to the time and space of work. While one can measure the productivity of manual labor performed in the assembly line by counting the number of items assembled in a given time, the problem of cognitive capitalism becomes that of measuring the cognitive labor performed by a scientist, an artist, a teacher, a designer, or a writer. Do they ever really stop working, that is, thinking? Furthermore, the notion of cognitive labor suggests that this type of value-creation is not confined to those who would be classed as "cognitive workers" from a sociological point of view, but affects the global mass of living labor—including activities performed in leisure time such as posting comments, photographs or videos to social networking platforms or inventing a new fashion style that only later will be picked up by the industry. For Christian Marazzi, the creation of value is thus increasingly unlinked from direct processes of production, spreading through externalized networks ranging "from outsourcing to crowdsourcing": "We work for free any moment of the day, there is a continuous transfer of unpaid labor onto the consumer. We can think about the banking system with online banking, the postal system, not to talk about IKEA (which forces you to assemble everything yourself at home) or Google."[7] Consumption as such is increasingly identified as constituting a creative activity actualizing new worlds by socializing tastes, values, and judgments. More radically, according for example to Maurizio Lazzarato, the end of the hegemony and centrality of factory work to the accumulation of value implies a crisis of political economy reactualizing the potential of a neo-Tardean "economic psychology" that reveals the underlying social nature of value.[8] As a result, it is argued that contemporary capitalism is characterized by a strong tension between the social features of production and the private character of accumulation. Inasmuch as the private character of accumulation tends to destroy the immaterial commons of knowledge required by this type of economy, it enacts a self-destructive cycle. As an economy of debt and austerity displaces the economy of credit that fueled the digital economy of the nineties and aughts, we witness the "becoming rent of profit," evident in the increasing amount of surplus value generated by financialization, real estate speculation, and the enforcement of intellectual property regimes and copyright.[9]

From advertising and marketing to the biotech and pharmaceutical industries, from media production to the arts, from care of the body and the self (care of children, the elderly, the sick, beauty, and fitness) to the aesthetic production of everyday life (everything pertaining to the home, fashion, and style), ultimately, contemporary capitalism implies a real subsumption of the whole of life stretching from the biological life of the species to the spiritual life of publics, from bios to noos, from organic to inorganic life.[10] Real subsumption, however, should not be identified with complete domination, on the contrary. Cognitive capitalism is crossed by a constituent tension between the tendency toward exploitation, subsumption and proletarianization on one side, and autonomy, self-reference, and self-creation on the other.

As a concept aiming to politicize the notion of the knowledge economy from a post-workerist Marxist perspective, the notion of cognitive capitalism is not immune to critique. Identifying the source of value in the cognitive capacities of living labor belies an emphasis on the symbolic and the linguistic that underestimate the centrality of the affective and the pre-cognitive to the operations of contemporary capitalism and downplays the active role played by its technical machines. The notion of psychopathologies of cognitive capitalism in a way short-circuits such cognitivism by foregrounding unconscious and libidinal processes that disrupt the smooth productivity of cognitive production while at the same time stressing the problematic nature of the incorporation of the technical machine or fixed capital in the body of living labor. Attention deficit disorder, depression, anxiety, panic, burn-out syndrome, and even new quasi-pathologies such as internet addiction expose a kind of excess of the life of the psyche with relation to the imperatives of productivity.

It is not by chance, then, that the "neurological turn" identified by Anna Munster as characterizing a certain discourse around networked media increasingly displaces the centrality of the life sciences and artificial life in the nineties.[11] If nineties digital capitalism invested in the neo-evolutionary powers of production of biological life, the aughts witnessed a new investment in the sciences of the brain and the technologies of artificial intelligence. Thus on the one hand, as Catherine Malabou points out, the neuroplastic, flexible brain has come to provide a new image of networked capitalism,[12] while on the other hand, for Munster, research in artificial intelligence has "shifted away from the construction of human-machine intelligence and the goal of creating an artificially intelligent 'mind,' and over to 'practical' applications for industry and for the military: [...] 'smart applications' [...] such as electronic fraud detection, voice and face recognition and data mining systems."[13]

The rising powers of the "neuro-image" materialized through imaging technologies such as fMRI define the difference between the normal and the pathological as a function of brain activity while at the same time new ordinary technologies of artificial intelligence expose new capacities of inhuman assemblages to pay attention to the processes immanent to the productive powers of the social brain.[14] The definition of what constitutes psychopathology and its social generalization thus unfolds as part of a mode of power/knowledge which conceives the life of the psyche in terms which displace the centrality of repression, Oedipus and the unconscious structured like a language in favor of a technical and neuro-centric conception of the ordinary psychopathologies of the networked brain.

This knowledge of the brain, however, is far from constituting a kind of exclusive property of the neurosciences. From Deleuze and Guattari to Toni Negri, the brain, in fact, also constitutes a key concept for those philosophies that try to construct a materialist alternative to psychoanalysis. Gilles Deleuze and Félix Guattari famously argue that the molecular biology of the brain constitutes a better image of thought than the psychoanalytic unconscious.[15] Charles T. Wolfe also reconstructs what he calls a genealogy of the social brain, providing an historically materialist account of psychic life which stretches from the Spinozist parallelism of body and thought to Soviet psychologists' conceptualization of the socialist cortex and Toni Negri's statement that the brain is the main productive force or the Common.[16] Maurizio Lazzarato also dedicates a book to Gabriel Tarde's critique of political economy where the concept of the brain as both "society" of neural cells and as engine of material and immaterial production founds a new social "economic psychology" which is alternative both to orthodox Marxist political economy and to neoclassical economics.[17]

In the following pages, I will look briefly at two main examples of ordinary psychopathologies which respectively refer to a neuronal modification of the structure of the brain triggered by interaction with information and communication technologies: attention-deficit disorders and anhedonia (the inability to experience pleasure). Reflecting the enduring power of Canguilheim's analysis of the formation of the category of the normal and the pathological in contemporary nosology, such pathologies are defined both as quantitative variations "departing from the normal [...] by *hyper-* or *hypo-*" (as in the case of attention disorders) or as error (as in the case of anhedonia).[18] Looking at such pathologies from a post-autonomist perspective, however, allows us to deploy what we might almost describe as a "stratagematic" and "schizoanalytic" reading or a transformation of the assessment of the parameters at play.[19] It is not a question of building a comprehensive account of such psychopathologies, but of introducing some elements of problematization both in the neurological account of psychopathology and in critical accounts that tends to stress only the suffering experienced by the cognitariat in cognitive capitalism. "Hyper" or "too much" will thus be also read positively as excess, implicating that which cannot be completely absorbed by cognitive capitalism and which lingers as a remainder of what is not containable and subsumable within its logic. "Hypo" or "too little" and "absence" as error, will be read as a stratagem of subtraction, of flight from cognitive capitalism's capture with ambivalent political implications. Overall the purpose of this exercise will be to establish whether the link between psychopathology and the brain produces a reading which not only stresses the cost paid by the psyche to exploitation, but also its autonomous strategy of excess and subtraction pointing to the horizon of an autonomous, self-productive social brain. This is why this essay will not so much focus on explicitly pathologic forms of psychic suffering as much as on ordinary psychopathologies of cognitive capitalism.

(In)attentive

> *"Our lived relationship with the brain becomes increasingly fragile, less and less "Euclidean" and goes through little cerebral deaths. The brain becomes our problem or our illness, our passion rather than our mastery, our solution or decision."*
> — Gilles Deleuze, *Cinema 2: The Time Image*

In a comic strip, cult Italian cartoonist Zerocalcare describes what could be defined as an ordinary occurrence in the daily life of cognitive labor.[20] "Almost every night at home the eternal struggle is staged between, on the one side, the forces of good, life and joy, and, on the other side, the forces of work." It is almost nine in the evening and Zerocalcare needs to finish his drawings which must be submitted to the editor the following day. As he is considering not finishing his work in time for the deadline in order to indulge in other kinds of bodily pleasures, a kind of superego is evoked in the shape of former British Prime Minister Margaret Thatcher. Expressing the spirit of forced work under the pressure of competition, Thatcher threatens him with the example of the Chinese worker who never stops working and slaps away his other animal spirit who incites him to desertion. Giving in to the violence of Thatcher, Zerocalcare decides to work and switches on his computer with the intention of checking his email before starting with the assigned task. The next table sees him five hours later, at 2:15 in the morning, having been absorbed in what his animal spirit calls "the Bermuda timezone": "The Bermuda timezone is that span of time between 9 pm and 2 am where apparently normal people sit in front of the computer and within the time of an eye-blink realize that five hours have inexplicably passed, swallowed by a dense curtain of fog and oblivion, jeopardizing deadlines, exams, health [...]." As a result, Zerocalcare does not meet his deadline and must spend the rest of the night fighting off the vengeful and angry spirit of Margaret Thatcher.

One of the explanations that Zerocalcare gives himself (beyond having been drugged with Roipnol or kidnapped by aliens) is the existence of a hypnotic function within the Facebook chat, which is activated around that time. However, as his brain's long-term memory is short-circuited by what Sherry Turkle once described as "computer holding power," software is paying attention, accumulating a mass of micro-data about his interaction with the network.[21] A quick retrieval of the chronology on his web browser brings back unknown memories of aimless drifting from website to website chasing trivial information.

It is clear that what we are dealing with here is not so much the pathologization of attention in children and adolescents, but a kind of ordinary psychopathologization such as that identified by Nicholas Carr in his much quoted article "Why Google is Making Us Stupid" (later turned into a book *The Shallows*).[22] Such pathologization of attention is an ordinary occurrence in the life of cognitive capitalism, expressing not so much a clear boundary between the normal and the pathological as a modulation of a general pathologization of neural life which crucially implicates our symbiotic relation with digital screens. Citing neuroscientific research on neuroplasticity, Carr has argued that multitasking and "always on" connectivity produce an excess of stimulation of the regions of the brain associated with short-term memory, while downplaying and atrophying long-term memory. The notion of the neuroplasticity of the brain is thus drawn upon to emphasize the production, by means of computers and communication networks, of a subject incapable of long-term memory and as a consequence of focused concentration and rational argumentation.

As attention is identified in new economy discourse as the new scarce resource in an economy of information, a new "crisis of attentiveness" is produced. It has been the merit of Jonathan Crary's work on early capitalism to show how such crisis is far from being a new phenomenon.[23] It was in the late nineteenth century and early twentieth century that a crisis of attention was first denounced—

triggered by a new commercial, urban culture of sensory stimulation. Looking back at the first expansion of industrial capitalism into the structures of perception in the nineteenth century, Crary shows how "at the moment when the dynamic logic of capital began to dramatically undermine any stable or enduring structure of perception, this logic simultaneously attempted to impose a disciplinary regime of attentiveness."[24] In the late nineteenth century, it was the new field of scientific psychology that identified attention as a fundamental problem. Crary underlines how "the emergence of a social, urban, psyche, and industrial field increasingly saturated with sensory input" turned "inattention" into a "danger and a serious problem even though it was often the very modernized arrangements of labor that produced inattention." Crary thus points towards the "crisis of attentiveness" as a crucial aspect of modernity, something that is produced by the "changing configurations of capitalism." These changing configurations are described as first introducing "an endless sequence of new products, sources of stimulation, and streams of information" and then respond to ensuing crisis of attentiveness "with new methods for managing and regulating perception." However, "the articulation of a subject in terms of attentive capacities simultaneously disclosed a subject incapable of conforming to such disciplinary imperatives."[25] As a widespread, almost normal psychopathology, this hyper-attention and hypo-attention expresses what from the point of view of capital is both a limit and a new source of potential extraction of value. It indexes both a withdrawal and a subtraction from productivity as when employers complain of widespread use of social networking sites during working hours and at the same time a kind of excess of neural life, the life of the brain with relation to strategies of capture of value. If it is true that Zerocalcare's browsing history does produce data that is somehow turned into economic value by software such as Google's AdSense and AdWords, it is also true that advertisers, who at the beginning were convinced by the accuracy of Google's measure of attention, increasingly complain about the "degraded" quality of such attention.[26] In its ordinary pathologization, such a deficit of attention seems to characterize the entirety of living labor whether it acts in its capacity as waged work or as free labor. Unfocused workers do not perform well because multitasking and constant connectedness distracts them from scheduled work. Unfocused, drifting populations of potential customers browse the internet in a state of absorbed distraction, where the process of moving from site to site happens too quickly to extract more than a micro-rent. Read as a constituent strategy of resistance of the social brain to exploitation and subsumption, such ordinary pathologies of attention seem to imply the excess of a new kind of brain that unfolds in connection with its devices. Is there more of a hint of a "future social brain" unfolding within this dynamic process? Gabriel Tarde again famously drew on psychopathological phenomena such as hypnosis, "magnetization," and somnambulism to cast light on what he thought to be the most basic presupposition of the social: our inclination to be affected by others, "our constant openness to a plurality of suggestions."[27] And on what conditions and on the basis of what ongoing experiments can such hypnotic relation to technosociality be turned into a new technology of autonomous self-creation such as the one wished for by Félix Guattari in his conceptualization of the post-media age?[28]

Anhedonia

> "What can we do so that the break-through does not become a breakdown?"
> — Gilles Deleuze

On an autumn day of 2012, during a particularly intense season of struggles by precarious cognitive labor in Rome, Italy, a series of billboards appeared plastered all over the walls of a neighborhood popular with the cognitariat, Il Pigneto. In striking red, yellow and black, the signs read: "Enough with rising drug prices": "Psychoactive substances are a tool of synthonization and synchronization of the precarious and intermittent times of life and work [...]." Referring to the examples highlighted in the poster, such as "the 12% rise in the price of cocaine, 20% for marijuana, 25% for MDMA, and 16% for heroin," the poster states that "rising prices for such substances are an indiscriminate attack on the bare life of the working class." Countering the "prescriptive regimen of the dose" with the "illicit regimen of the hit," this provocative media campaign of the Italian cognitariat draws on the importance of the modulation not only of attention but also of pleasure and desire to the life of cognitive labor.[29]

As Matthew Fuller and Andrew Goffey point out, "the development of psychopharmacology and its steady infection of the social generates new media spaces, new media with their own messages."[30] When talking about the psychopathologies of cognitive capitalism, then, one should not underestimate the powers not only of "electronic technologies working at a distance in extended space but chemical technologies creating distances in intensive space." The result is a psychotopology of the techno-social brain "meshing with the loops and hits of online connectivity, catalyzing circulation through the topologies of networks linking synapses, minds, emotions, techno-science, geopolitics, creating grey media for grey matter and vice versa."[31] The ordinary, normative character of pleasure and desire, their relation to the neurochemical composition of the brain and the potential of a new psychopharmacological solution to libidinal disinvestment in economic behavior is central to a video posted on YouTube by a young neuroscientist from Stanford University, Brian Knuston.[32] Posing the question of desire from the perspective of science, rather than philosophy, the neuroscientist asks of desire functional questions such as: "What are the neural substrates that support desire, when does it happen, what are the conditions for it to emerge, and is it good for anything? Is it good for making decisions for instance? And is it also important for our well-being?" The question of desire, the conditions for its emergence, and its value are posed from the point of view of a normal subject capable of performing economic decisions and imply also the emergence of an abnormal subject, the schizophrenic-anhedonic, unable to mobilize it. The two researches are presented as intrinsically distinct but overlapping inasmuch as research into the neurological basis of decision-making also, almost incidentally, indicates a possible program of development of new pharmaceutical drugs curing schizophrenia and depression. Through a kind of neuro-economic reductivism, psychiatric diseases are said to be caused by "disorders in decision-making" and can be addressed by neurochemically targeting those regions of the brain responsible for "rational" decision-making. The concluding remarks give us a sense of the axioms of this specific piece of research: brain activation reflects desire and predicts financial choice, while also indexing health symptoms. On this basis, neuroeconomics can be used to build "a comprehensive theory of decision making that can account for the wide spread of decisions that people make both when they are rational and reflective and when they are not."

The bulk of the experiment concerns what the neuroscientist describes as "a scientific enquiry into desire," which revolves around the study of neurological excitement as anticipation and intention. Having defined desire as that which motivates decisions and anticipation as an "evoker" or "sign" of desire, the researcher demonstrates that the anticipation of making money or deciding to buy something activates the same region of the brain as that discovered in laboratory rats in a famous experiment from 1954 performed by James Millner and Peter Olds. The original research experiment was part of a larger, Cold War, behaviorist scientific effort to implement strategies of mind control at a distance. The setup of the project involved, in fact, an attempt to control the behavior of a rat (waking it up) by means of an electrode in the brain. The failure of the original experiment produced an interesting result: it isolated a subcortical region of the brain that reacted to stimulation.

Overturning the original experiment, rather than trying to control the behavior of the rat at a distance, Millner and Olds decided to let the rat control its own brain—even if in a limited and controlled manner. They let the rat access a lever which could be pressed at its own will. The result was remarkable: "The rat kept doing it on and on and on, did not stop. The rat would rather do this than sleep, eat, drink and have sex (that is, perform basic biological functions)."[33]

Knuston's experiment into the visualization of desire (that is, the construction of a neuro-image able to plot the activation of different regions of the brain) shows activation or lack of activation of a region of the brain not too far from that identified by Millner and Olds in 1954, but with improved temporal and spatial resolution thanks to advances in fMRI technologies. This time it is not so much a question of giving the experimental subject access to his own stimulation, but of finding an external stimulant able to activate the region of the brain connected with pleasure and hence with anticipation, intention and ultimately choice. The best stimulant, it turns out, is money: as Knuston puts it in the video, money can become an optimal experimental tool inasmuch as it not only "motivates" people (for example, to work), but also because of its reversibility (you can give it and take it away) and scalability (you can modulate the exact amount involved). It also allows researchers to map precisely what Knuston describes as the "most ubiquitous economic decisions out there," which is "investing money or purchasing products." The subjects of the experiment are wired up to a computer and asked to make investment decisions by clicking on a button. A lag is introduced between the time of the decision and the time of the outcome allowing the plotting of the pre-cognitive, affective reaction of the brain to the stimulation. The research shows how anticipation of making a large amount of money (relative to the experimental subject's income) activates the same region of the brain that caused the rat to lose interest in vital functions such as sex, food, drink and sleep. Activity in the same region is also shown to occur when facing the decision to purchase a commodity with a given price.

The conclusions drawn by the neuroscientist are startling from the point of view of the pathologization of neural life in cognitive capitalism. As Deleuze and Guattari point out, the distribution of the rational and irrational in a given society does not express a universally valid distinction, but is specific to its axiomatics. It corresponds to a division of interest and desire that experiments such as this somehow enact. The behavior of the rat that, given access to its own brain, unfailingly chooses to stimulate it at the expense of its own survival casts a dark shadow on the "normal" behavior of the stock market broker involved in making neuro-chemically-fired choices triggered by anticipation of massive future gain.

On the other hand, if the behavior of the economic investor is normalized as expressing a standardized relation between anticipation and gain which allows for functional economic behavior, the lack of activation of such a region is explicitly linked to a pathology that is described as a kind of anti-economic behavior, schizophrenia. "Schizophrenics are said to be suffering a lack of desire, negative symptoms, include anhedonia and lack of motivation. Some medications tend to make this symptom worse, others do not."[34] Wired up in the same way, schizophrenics could still perform economic decisions that rewarded them with money, but showed no activation of the "money spot," that is, no investment of desire. Schizophrenia is thus re-coded as a disorder of desire, an error causing a lack of activation that threatens the functioning of the normal, functional neuro-economic brain. Treating them with "a-typical" neuroleptics targeting those regions of the brain restored them to the normality of functional economic behavior.

In critical and philosophical terms, there is, as one should expect, a reduction of desire as a productive, connective, open process of world-creation to an economy of pleasure "as a repressive (negating) power."[35] In this sense, the experiment confirms current critiques of subjectivation in networked media, such as those proposed by Jodi Dean and Bernard Stiegler, who see the latter as decomposing and destroying desire by dissipating it into the reproductive circuits of communicative capitalism and thus creating "disassociated milieus" of trans-individuation.[36] The experiment can thus be seen as practically enacting the decomposition of libidinal energy in networked communication whereby users' participation is reduced to a sterile act of consumption for which the subject is paid in worthless "tiny nuggets of pleasure."[37]

What is pathologized seems only an error causing a subtraction, that is, a lack of or refusal to feel pleasure that belongs to schizophrenics and turns them into disordered subjects. But what is exorcised is also the excess that is built into the reward-oriented behavior of economic subjects: the self-destructive behavior of the wired rat. Furthermore, techno-social economic decision-making in stock markets enacts not so much the aggregate behavior of individual economic agents, but also affective contagion and the inhuman speed of digital technologies. As it has recently been pointed out, since at least 2006 a "robot-phase transition," triggered by technologies such as high frequency trading, has seen the "the quantity of robot-robot interactions in stock markets operating at millisecond speed [exceeding] that of human-robot interactions"—negating both the anthropocentric and individualistic model of economic behavior.[38] Rats, electrodes, imaging technologies, plots, computers, artificial intelligences and human subjects are linked in a chain which enacts the irrationality of capitalist ratio. What in the rat is pathological becomes rational for the economic investor. Even as the market is posed as the topos of a self-regulating, rational system, its rationality is exposed as connected to anticipation, the neurochemical hit of reward, and the autonomous power of runaway artificial intelligences. The resulting picture, rather than confirming the assumptions of neuroeconomics on the nature of human behavior, seems rather to disclose a collective capitalist brain exposed not simply to the occasional and random catastrophe or "black swan event," but, haunted by "little cerebral deaths," that is "frequent black swans events with ultrafast duration."[39]

On the other hand, is it possible to see, once again, in schizophrenia, and specifically in the singular element identified as pathological from the point of view of neuroeconomics, that is anhedonia, a symptom of withdrawal from the circuits of communicative capitalism? Do such experiments unwillingly point out the limits to the functioning of capitalism in forms of libidinal disinvestment not simply in money-making, but more generally in the subjective rewards promised by cognitive capitalism as a measure of success? Would the anhedonic position be exemplified in the growing number of NEETs (Not in Education, Employment or Training)? Can the lack of interest and anticipation experienced by anhedonic subjects turn into a more general disinvestment in the figure of *homo economicus*, entrepreneur of oneself, agent of economic decision-making at the expense of all else?

While the identification of schizophrenia as lack of desire can be read as a line of flight from the relentlessly reductive figure of *homo economicus*, it also seems reductive in this case to read these two figures in terms of a neat opposition. Gilles Deleuze, summarizing his work with Félix Guattari on schizophrenia and the unconscious, presents the former as a condition where a struggle takes place between two poles: an exacerbated working of the machines (a non-organic functioning of the organ-machines) and a catatonic stasis—"[a]ll the phases of this struggle [...] translated in the type of anxiety which is specific to the schizophrenic."[40] Neuroeconomic experiments such as the one explained above seem to confine schizophrenia as lack or error only to the second condition (lack of pleasure or the catatonic body), while in fact normalizing the "exacerbated workings of the machine" at work in the social brain of financial capital. Creating a binary opposition between the functional and ordered economic subject (socially translated as the investor) and the dysfunctional and disordered schizophrenics (socially translatable into the NEETs), such experiments dismiss the mutual powers of contamination of these two struggling poles: "there is always some stimulus or impulse stealing into the heart of the catatonic stupor; and vice versa, stupor and rigid stasis are forever creeping over the swarming machines [...]."[41] Deleuze suggests that opening up the schizophrenic process in such a way as to counteract those strategies of normalization which employ chemical or institutional means to literally "lock the schizophrenic up" requires a combination of "lived chemistry" and "schizological analysis."[42] As he also asks, what kind of group, what kind of collectivity would be required to turn the catatonic body and the hyper-machinic body into something else? As the milieus of individuation, that is the conditions by which new kinds of subjectivities can be formed, are increasingly defined by the powers of corporate networked media, what kind of social brain can be materialized to unleash a new "molecular revolution" arising from libidinal disinvestment in the rewards of cognitive capitalism?

4

Red Stack Attack! Algorithms, Capital and the Automation of the Common[1]

(2014)

At stake in the following is the relationship between "algorithms" and "capital"— that is, the increasing centrality of algorithms "to organizational practices arising out of the centrality of information and communication technologies stretching all the way from production to circulation, from industrial logistics to financial speculation, from urban planning and design to social communication."[2] How should we grasp the relation between algorithms, processes of valorization of users' activities in networked digital media, and possibilities for emancipation from capital's stronghold over social cooperation? Are algorithms inevitably bonded to forms of control as regulations that are incompatible with any postcapitalist mode of production? Should they ever be considered part of efforts to exit neoliberal capitalism? If the concept of the common refers to "the product of [...] forms of governing and social co-operation," as opposed to simply "an intrinsic feature of the nature of particular categories of goods," as in the notion of the commons, how can we reclaim self-governance and networked, techno-social cooperation from capitalist enclosure and rent?[3]

We could start with considering how algorithms, those apparently esoteric computational structures, have become part of the daily life of users of contemporary digital and networked media. Digital network users are subjected to the power of algorithms every day: Google's PageRank (which sorts the results of search queries) or Facebook's EdgeRank (which automatically decides the order in which we should see news on our feeds), for example, not to mention the many other lesser-known algorithms (Appinions, Klout, Hummingbird, PKC, Perlin noise, Cinematch, KDP Select, and many more) that modulate our relationships with data, digital devices, and each other. This widespread presence of algorithms in the daily life of digital culture, however, is only one of the expressions of the pervasiveness of computational techniques as they become increasingly coextensive with processes of production, consumption, and distribution displayed in logistics, finance, architecture, medicine, urban planning, infographics, advertising, dating, gaming, publishing, and all kinds of creative expression (music, graphics, dance, and so on).

The staging of the encounter between algorithms and capital as a political problem invokes the possibility of breaking the spell of capitalist realism—that is, the idea that capitalism constitutes the only possible way to organize our productive activities while at the same time claiming that new ways of organizing the production and distribution of wealth need to seize on scientific and technological developments.[4] Going beyond the opposition between state and market, or public and private, the concept of the common is used here as a way to instigate the thought and practice of a possible postcapitalist mode of existence for social cooperation in networked digital media.

Algorithms, Capital and Automation

Discussions about the potential of computational networks in enabling a postcapitalist economy tend to revolve around concepts of the commons or the common. Writings about commons-based peer production tend to privilege the notion of commons as a good, mostly drawing on Elinor Ostrom's framework, thus suggesting that peer production is primarily enabled by the specific character of information as a nonrival good—a good that can be enjoyed in common.[5] In his early essay about "peer production," for example, Yochai

Benkler draws a difference between "commons-based peer production" and "peer production" as involving a difference in regimes of property. Peer production, for Benkler, refers to "instances of socially productive behavior" or "large- and medium-scale collaborations among individuals that are organized without markets or managerial hierarchies."[6] He characterizes commons-based peer production in the classic terms provided by literature on natural commons, and redeploys them to deal with knowledge commons: "non-proprietary regimes" or "absence of exclusion"; whether the use of the commons is open to anybody in the world or limited; whether it is self-regulated or not; according to the means of provisioning and allocating resources. Theorists of the common, however, argue that in Ostrom's theory of the commons "what remains as a central element defining common goods is the particular nature of certain goods, in continuity with the ahistorical and static approach to classification of goods (private, public, common, belonging to a club) driven by neo-classical inspired economic theory."[7] Drawing on Michael Hardt and Antonio Negri, Carlo Vercellone and his co-authors argue that the common is the "socially and historically determinate activity that incessantly produces new institutions, which are at the same time the conditions and result of 'common' itself."[8] As such, while the notion of the commons is dependent on a classification of different types of goods (private, public, and common), the concept of the common refers to "cognitive labor and knowledge [...] as the common element that establishes and renders possible the social structure of any type of commons, independently of the nature of the goods, whether they be material or immaterial, subject to the constraints of scarcity or abundant."[9] Thus for theorists of the common, the matter is not identifying which goods seem to qualify best for "commons-based peer production," but how the common as a political concept indicates the centrality of bio-cognitive labor and social cooperation to value production and the necessity of conceiving new political horizons that acknowledge the increasingly social nature of production in ways that reward and sustain it.

Looking at algorithms from a perspective that seeks the constitution of a new political rationality around the concept of the common means engaging with the ways in which algorithms are deeply implicated in the changing nature of automation. If what Vercellone, Fumagalli, and others call "bio-cognitive capitalism" intensifies the cooperative nature of labor, then algorithms become signs of a new mode of automation with relation to the industrial model described by Marx. Marx describes automation as a process of absorption into the machine of the "general productive forces of the social brain," such as "knowledge and skills" that therefore appear as an attribute of capital rather than as the product of social labor.[10] Looking at the history of capital and technology, it is clear how automation has evolved away from the thermo-mechanical model of the early industrial assembly line toward the electro-computational, dispersed networks of contemporary capitalism. Hence it is possible to read algorithms as part of a genealogical line that, as Marx put it in his "Fragment on Machines," started with the adoption of technology by capitalism as fixed capital, then pushed the former through several metamorphoses "whose culmination is the machine, or rather, an automatic system of machinery [...] set in motion by an automaton, a moving power that moves itself."[11] The industrial automaton was clearly thermodynamic, and gave rise to a system "consisting of numerous mechanical and intellectual organs so that workers themselves are cast merely as its conscious linkages."[12] It implied a cognitive division of labor within the factory, where organizational knowledge was the exclusive domain of white-collar workers, while blue-collar workers toiled on the factory floor—and the reproductive work of women went unacknowledged.[13] The digital automaton, however, is electro-computational: it "puts the soul to work," it primarily involves the nervous system and the brain, it comprises "possibilities of virtuality, simulation, abstraction, feedback and autonomous processes," and it does not presuppose a gendered division between productive and reproductive work, even as it engenders its own modes of sexualization.[14] The digital automaton unfolds in networks consisting of electronic and nervous connections so that users themselves are cast as quasi-automatic relays of a ceaseless information flow. It is in this wider assemblage, then, that algorithms need to be located when discussing new modes of automation.

Quoting a textbook of computer science, Andrew Goffey describes algorithms as "the unifying concept for all the activities which computer scientists engage in [...] and the fundamental entity with which [they] operate."[15] An algorithm can be provisionally defined as the "description of the method by which a task is to be accomplished" by means of sequences of steps or instructions that operate according to data and computational structures. As such, an algorithm is an abstraction "having an autonomous existence independent of what computer scientists like to refer to as 'implementation details,' that is, its embodiment in a particular programming language for a particular machine architecture."[16] It can vary in complexity from the most simple set of rules described in natural language (such as those used to generate coordinated patterns of movement in smart mobs) to the most complex mathematical formulas involving all kinds of variables (as in the famous Monte Carlo algorithm used to solve problems in nuclear physics, which was later applied to stock markets and now to the study of nonlinear technological diffusion processes). At the same time, in order to work, algorithms must exist as parts of assemblages that include hardware, data, data structures (such as lists, databases, and memory), and the behaviors and actions of bodies. For the algorithm to become social software, in fact, "it must gain its power as a social or cultural artifact and process by means of a better and better accommodation to behaviors and bodies which happen on its outside."[17] Furthermore, for Luciana Parisi, the ingression of the logic of computation into culture marks the transformation of algorithms from "instructions to be performed" into "performing entities." This transformation is linked to the "entropic tendency of data to increase in size," which causes "infinite amounts of information [to] interfere with and re-program algorithmic procedures."[18] For Parisi, this "new function of algorithms thus involves not the reduction of data to binary digits, but the ingression of random quantities into computation." Hence, algorithms are neither a homogeneous set of techniques, nor do they guarantee "the infallible execution of automated order and control."[19] They do not simply correspond to a new mode of "algorithmic regulation" that ensures the smooth optimization of all kinds of processes, but confront governance with "data that produce alien rules," rules that are "at once discrete and infinite, united and fractalized."[20] Or, as theorists of the common would put it, when algorithms meet the infinite data produced by social cooperation, they do not achieve a smooth control but are confronted with an excess, that is, a surplus, which causes the capitalist governance of bio-cognitive labor to face new indeterminacies.

From the point of view of capitalism, on the other hand, algorithms are mainly a form of fixed capital—they are just means of production. They encode a certain quantity of social knowledge (abstracted from that elaborated by mathematicians, programmers, and also users' activities), but they are not valuable per se. In the current economy, they are valuable only inasmuch as they allow for the conversion of knowledge into exchange value (monetization) and its exponentially increasing accumulation (the titanic quasi-monopolies of the corporate Stack). Insofar as they constitute fixed capital, algorithms such as Google's PageRank and Facebook's EdgeRank appear "as a presupposition against which the value-creating power of the individual labor capacity is an infinitesimal, vanishing magnitude," and that is why calls for individual retributions to users for their "free labor" are misplaced.[21] What needs to be foregrounded is not the individual work of the user, but the much larger powers of social cooperation thus unleashed. This implies a profound transformation of the grip that the social relation that we call the capitalist economy has on society.

From the point of view of capital, algorithms are fixed capital, assets that work as means of production finalized to achieve an economic return. But, like all technologies and techniques, that is not all they are. Marx explicitly states that, even though capital appropriates technology as the most effective form of the subsumption of labor, this is not all that can be said about it. Its existence as machinery, he insists, is not "identical with its existence as capital [...] and therefore it does not follow that subsumption under the social relation of capital is the most appropriate and ultimate social relation of production for the application of machinery."[22] It is then essential to remember that the instrumental value that algorithms have for capital does not exhaust the value of technology in general and algorithms in particular—that is, their capacity to express not just "use value" as Marx put it, but also aesthetic, existential, social, and ethical values. We need to ask, then, not only how algorithmic automation works today (mainly in terms of control, monetization, and feeding the debt economy), but also what kind of time and energy it subsumes, and how it might be made to work by different social and political assemblages that are not completely subsumed by or subjected to the capitalist drives toward accumulation and exploitation.

Contrary to some variants of Marxism that tend to identify technology completely with "fixed capital," "dead labor," or "instrumental rationality," and hence with control and capture, it is important to remember how, for Marx, the evolution of machinery also indexes a level of development of productive powers that are unleashed but never totally contained by the capitalist economy. What interested Marx (and what makes his work still relevant to those who strive for a postcapitalist mode of existence) is the way in which, so he claims, the tendency of capital to invest in technology to automate and hence reduce its labor costs to a minimum potentially frees up a surplus of time and energy (labor), or an excess of productive capacity. However, what characterizes a capitalist economy is that this surplus of time and energy is not simply released, but must be constantly reabsorbed in the cycle of production of exchange value, leading to the increasing accumulation of wealth by the few (the collective capitalist) at the expense of the many.

Automation, then, when seen from the point of view of capital, must always be balanced with new ways to control (that is, absorb and exhaust) the time and energy released by it. It must produce poverty and stress when there should be wealth and leisure. It must make market price the measure of value, even when it is apparent that science, technology, and social cooperation constitute the source of the wealth produced. It thus inevitably leads to the periodic and widespread destruction of this accumulated wealth, in the form of psychic burn-out, environmental catastrophe, and physical destruction of wealth through war. It creates hunger where there should be satiety; it puts food banks next to the homes of the super-rich. That is why the notion of a postcapitalist mode of existence must become believable, that is, it must become what Maurizio Lazzarato described as an enduring autonomous focus of subjectivation.[23] What a postcapitalist common can aim for is not only a better distribution of wealth compared to the unsustainable one that we have today, but also a reclaiming of disposable time—the time and energy freed from work to be deployed in developing and complicating the very notion of what is necessary. This disposable time is a key component of an economy organized around the "common in the singular."[24] This could constitute a revitalization of the tradition of "red cybernetics," outlined, for example, by Nick Dyer-Witheford and Eden Medina, in ways which relink communism to democracy, freedom, and the respect for singularities that were previously foreclosed by the socialist planner state.[25]

The history of capitalism has shown that automation as such has not reduced the quantity and intensity of labor demanded by managers and capitalists. On the contrary, as far as technology is only a means of production to capital, where it has been able to deploy other means, it has not innovated. For example, industrial technologies of automation in the factory do not seem to have recently experienced any significant technological breakthroughs. Most industrial labor today is still heavily manual, automated only in the sense of being hooked up to fast electronic networks of prototyping, marketing, and distribution; and it is rendered economically sustainable only by political means—by exploiting geopolitical and economic differences (arbitrage) on a global scale, and by controlling migration flows through new technologies of the border.[26] The state of things in most industries today is intensified exploitation, which produces an impoverished mode of mass production and consumption that is damaging to the body, subjectivity, social relations, and the environment. As Marx put it, disposable time released by automation should allow for a change to the very essence of the human, so that the new subjectivity is allowed to return to the performing of necessary labor in such a way as to redefine what is necessary beyond the limits of predefined needs and motivations.

The notion that the common is a mode of production, then, does not imply that we should return to simpler times by defining the real basic needs that we need to satisfy, but, on the contrary, a matter of acknowledging that growing food and feeding populations, constructing shelter and adequate housing, learning and researching, caring for children, the sick, and the elderly, facing the challenges of climate change, composting with the critters with whom we share the planet, choosing one's forms of spirituality (a relation to the forces of subjectification that exceed oneself), pursuing the endless struggle for freedom requires the mobilization of social invention and cooperation.[27] The whole process can be transformed from a process of production for the few by the many, steeped in impoverishment and stress, to one where the many redefine the meaning of what is necessary and valuable, while inventing new ways of achieving it.

For Andrea Fumagalli and Carlo Vercellone, for example, the foregrounding of social cooperation as the source of value and wealth requires new institutions that they call "Commonfare" as a mode of reappropriation and reinvention of the old and mostly now inadequate institutions of the welfare state. The construction of the institutions of Commonfare require for Vercellone not the action of a centralized state, but "the socialization of investment and money and the question of the modes of management and organization which allow for an authentic democratic reappropriation of the institutions of Welfare [...] and the ecologic re-structuring of our systems of production."[28]

The Red Stack: Virtual Money, Social Networks, Bio-hypermedia

In his 2012 lecture at the Berlage Institute, later developed in his book *The Stack: On Software and Sovereignty*, digital media and political theorist Benjamin H. Bratton argues that we are witnessing the emergence of a new nomos of the earth, where older geopolitical divisions linked to territorial sovereign powers are intersecting with the new nomos of the internet and new forms of sovereignty extending in electronic space.[29] This new heterogeneous nomos involves the overlapping of national governments (China, United States, European Union, Brazil, Egypt, and others), transnational bodies (the IMF, the WTO, the European Banks, and NGOs of various types), and corporations (Google, Facebook, Apple, and Amazon), producing differentiated patterns of mutual accommodation marked by moments of conflict. Drawing on the organizational structure of computer networks or "the OSI network model, upon which the TCP/IP stack and the global internet itself is indirectly based," Bratton develops the concept and/or prototype of the "stack" to define the features of "a possible new nomos of the earth linking technology, nature and the human."[30] The stack supports and modulates a kind of "social cybernetics" able to compose "both equilibrium and emergence." As a "megastructure," the stack implies

> a confluence of interoperable standards-based complex material-information systems of systems, organized according to a vertical section, topographic model of layers and protocols [...] composed equally of social, human and "analog" layers (chthonic energy sources, gestures, affects, user-actants, interfaces, cities and streets, rooms and buildings, organic and inorganic envelopes) and informational, non-human computational and "digital" layers (multiplexed fiber optic cables, datacenters, databases, data standards and protocols, urban-scale networks, embedded systems, universal addressing tables).[31]

In this section, drawing on Bratton's political prototype, I would like to propose the concept of the "red stack"— that is, a new nomos for the post-capitalist common. I will start by proposing at least three layers of the red stack, which remains, however, a modular structure with its own inde-terminacies and virtualities. These layers are: vir-tual money, social networks, and bio-hypermedia. These three levels, although "stacked," that is, layered, are to be understood as interacting trans-versally and nonlinearly. They constitute a possible way to think about an infrastructure of autono-mization linking together technology and sub-jectivation.

Virtual Money

The contemporary economy, as Christian Marazzi and others argue, is founded on a form of money ("fiat money") which has been turned into a series of signs with no fixed referent (such as gold) to anchor them, explicitly dependent on the compu-tational automation of simulational models, screen media with automated displays of data (indexes, graphics, and so on), and algo-trading (bot-to-bot transactions) as its emerging mode of automa-tion.[32] Such money is mainly emitted (like the sign it is) as a result of expectations of future revenues which, expanding into indeterminate futures, are allowed to increase to enormous size. As Robert

Meister argues, the liquidity of financial markets is ultimately dependent on government bonds, with national governments becoming the "lenders of last resort," which ensures that monetary production can continue by enforcing debt repayment from a nation's citizens in the form of cuts to public services and wages, foreclosures, and taxation. Our capacity to assume debt, for Meister, is becoming almost as important as our labor for the purposes of creating the vehicles for capital accumulation.[33]

As Antonio Negri also puts it, "money today— as abstract machine—has taken on the peculiar function of supreme measure of the values extracted out of society in the real subsumption of the latter under capital."[34] Since ownership and control of capital-money (which is different, as Maurizio Lazzarato reminds us, from wage-money, in its capacity to be used not only as a means of exchange, but as a means of investment, empowering certain futures over others) is crucial to maintaining populations bonded to the current power relation, how could we turn financial money into the money of the common? With the invention of cryptocurrencies, with all its limitations and problematic turns, "the taboo on money has been broken," opening up the possibility of thinking about money as something that can be programmed and designed.[35] Beyond its current expressions, the possibility remains of a future relation between the algorithms of money-creation and "a constituent practice which affirms other criteria for the measurement of wealth, valorizing new and old collective needs outside the logic of finance."[36] Attempts to develop new kinds of cryptocurrencies must be judged, valued, and rethought on the basis of this simple question, as posed by Andrea Fumagalli: is the currency created not limited solely to being a means of exchange, but can it also affect the entire cycle of money creation, from finance to exchange?[37] Does it allow speculation and hoarding, or does it promote investment in postcapitalist projects and facilitate freedom from exploitation and autonomy of organization? What is becoming increasingly clear is that algorithms will need to be an essential part of the process of creation of the money of the common, that is of a currency that accounts for and supports the value(s) produced by social cooperation. In this sense, money-creation algorithms also have politics. (What are the gendered politics of individual "mining," for example, and of the complex technical knowledge, machinery and environmental costs implied in mining Bitcoins?) The drive to completely automate money production in order to escape the fallacies of subjective factors and social relations has caused such relations to come back in the form of speculative trading. In the same way as financial capital is intrinsically linked to a certain kind of subjectivity (the financial predator typically narrated by Hollywood cinema), so an autonomous form of money needs to be both jacked into and productive of a new kind of subjectivity—not limited to the hacking milieu as such, and oriented not toward monetization and accumulation, but toward the empowering of social cooperation.

Other questions that designing the money of the common might involve are: by what means can we subtract money from the circuit of capitalist accumulation and turn it into money able to finance the institutions of Commonfare in the areas of education, research, health, environment, and so on? What are the lessons to be learned from crowdfunding models and their limits in thinking about new forms of financing autonomous projects of social cooperation?[38] How can we perfect and extend experiments such as that carried out by the Inter-Occupy movement during Hurricane Katrina, in turning social networks into crowdfunding networks that can then be used as logistical infrastructure able to move not only information, but also physical goods?[39]

Social Networks

Over the past ten years, digital media have undergone a process of becoming social that has introduced genuine innovation in relation to previous forms of social software (mailing lists, forums, multi-user domains, and so on). If mailing lists, for example, drew on the communication language of sending and receiving, social networking sites and the diffusion of (proprietary) social plug-ins have turned the social relation itself into the content of new computational procedures. When sending and receiving a message, we can say that algorithms operate outside the social relation as such, in the space of the transmission and distribution of messages; but social networking software intervenes directly in the social relation. Indeed, digital technologies and social networking sites "cut into" the social relation itself—that is, they turn it into a discrete object and introduce a new supplementary relation.[40] If, along with Gabriel Tarde and Michel Foucault, we understand the social relation as an asymmetrical relation involving at least two poles (one active and the other receptive) and characterized by a certain degree of freedom and potential for reversibility, we can think of actions such as liking and being liked, writing and reading, looking and being looked at, tagging and being tagged, and even buying and selling as the kind of conducts that transindividuate the social (they induce the passage from the preindividual through the individual to the collective). In social media, these actions become discrete technical objects (like buttons, comment boxes, and tags), which are then linked to underlying data structures (for example, the social graph) and subjected to the power of algorithmic ranking and machine learning. This produces the characteristic spatiotemporal modality of digital sociality today: the feed, an algorithmically customized flow of opinions, beliefs, statements, and desires expressed in words, images, sounds, and videos.

Much reviled in contemporary critical theory for their supposedly homogenizing effect, these new technologies of the social, however, also open the possibility of experimenting with many-to-many interaction and thus with the very processes of individuation. Techno-political experiments (see the various internet-based parties such as the Five Star Movement, the Pirate Party, Partido X, and Barcelona en Comú) draw on the powers of these new sociotechnical structures in order to produce massive processes of participation and deliberation; but, as with Bitcoin, they also show the far-from-resolved processes that link political subjectivation to algorithmic automation. They can function, however, because they draw on widely socialized new types of knowledge and crafts (how to construct a profile, how to cultivate a public, how to share and comment, how to make and post photos, videos, notes, GIFs, how to publicize events) and on "soft skills" of expression and relation (humor, argumentation, sparring) that are not implicitly good or bad, but present a series of affordances or degrees of freedom of expression for political action that cannot be left to capitalist monopolies. In this sense, it is not only a matter of using social media to organize resistance and revolt, but also a question of constructing a social mode of self-(in)formation, which can collect and reorganize existing drives toward autonomous and singular becomings. Given that algorithms, as we have said, cannot be unlinked from wider social assemblages, their materialization within the red stack involves overcoming the limits of social media as dominant technologies of collective subjectivation. If social media have given us the new dominant mode of production of the social, they have shown all their limits in their capacity to act as a distributed platform for learning about the world, nurturing new competences and skills, fostering planetary connections, and developing new ideas and values.

Bio-hypermedia

The term bio-hypermedia, coined by Giorgio Griziotti, identifies the ever-more intimate relation between bodies and devices that is part of the diffusion of smart phones, tablet computers, and ubiquitous computation. As digital networks shift away from the centrality of the desktop or even laptop toward smaller, more portable devices, a new social and technical landscape emerges around "apps" and "clouds," which directly "intervene in how we feel, perceive and understand the world."[41] Apps for platforms such as Android and Apple have been described as interfaces or membranes linking individual devices to large databases stored in the cloud (massive data processing and storage centers owned by large corporations).[42] This topological continuity has allowed for the diffusion of downloadable apps which increasingly modulate the relationship of bodies and space. Such technologies not only "stick to the skin and respond to the touch" (as Bruce Sterling once put it), but create new "zones" around bodies that now move through coded spaces overlaid with information, able to locate other bodies and places within interactive, informational visual maps. New spatial ecosystems emerging at the crossing of the "natural" and the "artificial" allow for the activation of a process of chaosmotic co-creation of urban life.[43] Here again we can see how apps are, for capital, simply a means to monetize and accumulate data about the body's movement while subsuming it ever more tightly in networks of consumption and surveillance. However, this subsumption of the mobile body under capital does not necessarily imply that its subsumption is the only possible use of these new technological affordances. Turning bio-hypermedia into components of the red stack (the mode of reappropriation of fixed capital in the age of the networked techno-social) implies drawing together current experimentation with hardware (from Shenzhen phone-hacking technologies to Indian jugaad to maker movements) able to support a new breed of "imaginary apps" (for example, the apps devised by the artist collective Electronic Disturbance Theater, which are designed to help migrants bypass border controls, or other apps able to track the origin of commodities and their degrees of exploitation).

Conclusions

This chapter proposes another strategy for the construction of a machinic infrastructure of the common. The basic idea is that information technologies, which comprise algorithms as a central component, do not simply constitute a tool of capital, but are simultaneously constructing new potentialities for post-neoliberal modes of government and postcapitalist modes of production. The possibility of doing this depends on opening possible lines of contamination along with the large movements of programmers, hackers, and makers involved in a process of recoding network architectures and information technologies based on values other than exchange and speculation. It also depends on acknowledging the wider technosocial literacy that has recently affected large swathes of the world population. It is a matter, then, of producing a convergence able to extend the problem of reprogramming the internet away from recent trends toward corporatization and monetization at the expense of users' freedom and control, linking bio-informational communication to issues such as the production of a money of the commons able to socialize wealth, against current trends toward privatization, accumulation, and concentration, and saying that social networks and diffused communicational competences can also function as means to organize cooperation and produce new knowledges and values. These would seek a new political synthesis that moves us away from the neoliberal paradigm of debt, austerity, and accumulation. This is not a utopia, but a program for the invention of constituent social algorithms of the common.

5

A Neomonadology of Social (Memory)
Production
(2016)

On the evening of the 7th of January 2015, a
crowd of over 100,000 people assembled in one of
the main squares of the city where I live and
work—the Mediterranean port of Naples in
southern Italy—for the funeral mass of Pino
Daniele, a beloved local musician who had been
overwhelmingly popular with his hybrid and soul-
ful version of Mediterranean blues.[1] His sudden
death due to a heart attack at the age of 59 had hit
the social networks first, as is increasingly the case
with celebrity deaths. A mass sharing of songs,
videos, and personal memories had flooded the
walls of Italian Facebook starting from the night of
the 5th, peaking on the 6th and the 7th, only to
quickly peter out when displaced by comments
and articles relating to the slaughter of the French
journalists of *Charlie Hebdo* in Paris.[2]

Standing in the silent and somber crowd, I
noticed how, when Daniele's most popular songs

sounded through the loudspeakers, the dark sea of people sparkled with the bright glow of thousands of small screens, which they lifted up to film and record the crowd softly singing along. Sri Lankan vendors criss-crossed the packed square with their latest street wares: extendable stick monopods made in China that allowed "group selfies" to be taken from above. The day before the funeral, photos and videos of a "flash mob" immediately summoned through the Facebook event page had also presented the same images of bright blue screens lighting up and filming a vast crowd of guitars and voices singing Daniele's songs in a spontaneous social memorial.

Watching both scenes, the first one live, the second one through my Facebook newsfeed, I couldn't help thinking that these acts of social memorization, which also entailed the social production and sharing of memories, were producing different types of "value." Undoubtedly they were producing some kind of value for the corporate owners of the social internet that registered as a local spike in activity, as views on YouTube, for example, which could be used to suggest new consumer propensities to algorithms, while they also raised the income streams of telecom operators, and provided free content for news outlets.[3] The event, in being just one of the many that agitate and animate transnational digital networks, pointed to the process whereby the generation of a social memory becomes a direct productive force in the economic domain. At the same time, an act such as this also genuinely produced what Marxists call "use values," values that are not consumed by marketization: a feeling of solidarity, social meaning, a moment of collective reflection, the sharing of memories producing a sense of belonging.[4] These "use values" could be further qualified in this case as a sense of beauty (aesthetic or cultural values such as the sound of Naples as a "black" European city) and of truth (truth values about one's life to which Daniele's songs had been a soundtrack or about the city and its history of interrupted modernity).[5] The scene I was witnessing was, of course, both *unique* in its singularity and *common*, as photographing, filming, recording, and sharing have become, thanks to digital technologies, a daily practice for many, thus constituting a new mode of social memorization. The production of economic value (exchange and utility), aesthetic and social values, technology and memory have become inextricably enmeshed. Remembering and sharing by technological means produces surplus value for the netarchical capitalists but also an excess of affects, desires, and beliefs materializing a "common ground."[6] This strange entanglement is enabled by technologies that, while constructing an undoubtedly social experience, read events such as this as predicated on the existence of a (social) network composed of individuals, but also exceeding both.

Two Tales of Social Production

There is a constitutive tension between the network (a diagram composed of nodes and links), the individual (the concept of the autonomous, rational subject) and the dividual (its datafied digital shadow) in that strange phenomenon called "social production" or "social cooperation," which both liberal and Marxist theories identify as a key source of the production of value in contemporary societies. Acts of social memorization such as the one presented above constitute just such a case of a larger continuum spanning the extremes of "mechanical" to "non-mechanical" cooperation, which Yochai Benkler calls "social" or "peer-to-peer (p2p) production." Theorists of social and peer-to-peer production register the efficacy of organizational strategies that enable individual autonomy and voluntary participation in the field of information and knowledge production. They explain social production as the result of the "falling costs of access to the means of production" coupled with the action of the "invisible hand of the social" enhanced by a peer-to-peer architecture or scale-free networks somehow harmonizing individual wills activated by social motivations.[7]

For theorists such as Benkler or Jeremy Rifkin, the key factor at work is internal to the movement of capital, so to speak: the falling costs of access to the capital needed to be an actor in the information economy allow for an amplification of the powers of decentralized individual action.[8] Benkler's notion of social production argues for the coordinate effects of noncoordinate actions inasmuch as one does not need to be consciously cooperating in order to be actually cooperating.[9] Just the act of recording and registering events of daily life and putting them online is enough to be cooperating from the point of view of the creation of economic value in a networked economy. For Benkler, the combination of individual social motivations and efficient coordination resolves "the tension between the values promoted by liberal markets and the values of liberal democracy."[10] A collective or social event which produces value brings together the individual capacity to choose, the social motivations which imply a kind of "peer pressure" on individual choice (such as acquiring social capital or standing with others), the consolidation of a feeling of similarity and belonging which constitutes society, and also the effect produced by a commercial network of smart devices which allows for memories to be registered as traces to be stored, tagged, classified, related and made available for current and future consumption. Technosocial memory thus starts as a series of actions (recording, uploading, tagging, posting, commenting, storing) which precipitate into digital objects producing value for the market and value for the social in what would appear as a seamless continuum that increases market value while consolidating social order.[11]

Post-workerist Marxists, on the other hand, following Marx's *Grundrisse*, argue instead that what they call social cooperation is not simply a new source of value, but the specific historical expression of living labor in an economy defined by the hegemony of immaterial value production and financialization. From this point of view, social cooperation is involved at every stage and throughout every layer of value-production in postindustrial economies, involving not simply the completion of a task and the reproduction of a template, but the production of new values and the socialization of invention. Daniele's music, emerging out of a proletarianized urban milieu ravaged by a crisis of industrialization, relied on the cooperation of a number of musicians and the reinvention of musical and cultural memories constituted by the social circulation of sounds, instruments, techniques, media, and rhythms in a transnational and transcontinental space spanning Europe, Africa, the Caribbean and North America.

The devices, protocols, platforms, and programming languages which allow for the storing and sharing of the products of such cooperation are the means through which the productive powers of living labor are appropriated and captured by contemporary capitalism—making rent and financialization the new dominant mode of extraction of surplus value.[12] The relational, linguistic and technological abilities released by post-Fordism become crucial components in the market-based production of value, but they can no longer be organized within the boundaries of the firm and the form of waged work. Inasmuch as it enacts a reappropriation of portions of fixed capital, this new source of value also retains an autonomous potential which is not exhausted or captured in advance by marketization. For post-workerist Marxists, this potential constitutes the (virtual) engine of a post-socialist and postcapitalist *com mon*, a co-poietic production which holds together the collective and the singular.[13] Here, as in Paolo Virno's adoption of Gilbert Simondon's philosophy, the common or social is the pre-individual (such as species-specific expressive capacities) and at the same time that reserve of being which allows the individual to undergo ever-new transformations.[14] It is the social memory of music but also the singularizing tendencies which each one brings to such memory and the new productions that it enables (including the production of new forms of social life).

Among the autonomist Marxists, however, nobody has gone as far as Maurizio Lazzarato in posing "autonomous and independent" social cooperation as the ontological and historical pre-supposition of economic valorization and the division of labor.[15] In particular, following Gabriel Tarde's critique in his *Economic Psychology* (1902), Lazzarato argues that monetization and the creation of social wealth depend on the primary flow of social currents which mobilize "mnemonic work" or the "labor of attention." The creation of value, from this perspective, depends only secondarily on capital and the division of labor, while resting primarily on the "cooperative dynamics of inter-cerebral psychological forces" which are not uni-laterally contained in the capital-labor relation. Cooperation, in fact, is social in so far as it is not founded on work or capital, but on the activity of the "spirit, soul, or memory."[16]

From this point of view, then, value is first of all a social production which is currently reconfigured by the digital networking of the social, by the ubiquitous social activity of recording, storing and sharing.[17] Theories of social production or cooperation also need to account for the series of elements included in an event such as the one described above: the individual holding up the digital device looking at the scene through the mobile screen; the simultaneous process of accumulation of audiovisual and linguistic digital traces recorded and stored in databanks and that constitute her at a micro-scale as a "dividual"; the social flow of currents of values which individuate the "common ground" of the crowd; the relational recursiveness of the network as digital objects are posted, shared and diffused; the multiplication of agencies at the technological level (screens, interfaces, protocols, programs, code, algorithms, bots, buttons etc.); and also the international and ethnic division of labor and the logistical arrangements that assemble the devices on the one hand, while on the other bring Southeast Asian traders to the streets of southern Europe.[18]

While Marxist theorists of social cooperation maintain the common and cooperation as the presupposition of economic valorization, liberal theories tend to emphasize the action of autonomous individuals—even as such actions at a collective level somehow obey a kind of mechanical coordination or even intrinsic social laws. If a networked society presents itself first of all as a "society of individuals," this is possibly also due to the ways in which devices are constructed as first of all "personal." The social life of digital media presents to us the recurring image of individual users interacting with their devices and the networked society comes across as "a 'society' of individual users connected by an information architecture."[19] Devices are constructed for individual use (desktops, laptops, tablets, smart phones) and individuals can be spotted in both public and private spaces staring or talking at their screen, shifting their attention in and out of their physical environment. The design of digital devices and interfaces mobilizes a "monadic" architecture of subjectivity, where "users" are individually enveloped by their devices in ways that allow them to abstract themselves periodically from their physical surroundings in order to engage in communicative acts. As Sherry Turkle put it, digital devices pose "being alone" as a "precondition for being together because it is easier to communicate if you can focus, without interruption on your screen."[20] Individual users "prehend" and are "prehended" by their devices including the network as a series of actions and relations (searching, clicking, opening, commenting, liking, posting, sharing, filming, photographing, reading, watching, "digging," blogging, sharing, chatting, listening, following, friending, etc.). As it unfolds itself in the network, the individual as singular "monad" is at the same time paradoxically "divided" in action constituting a digital double or "dividual."

Monadology and Digital Media

This relationship between irreducible singularity of the agent and the infinite divisibility of the ideal mathematical continuum is crucial to the set of problems that led the Baroque German philosopher Gottfried Wilhelm Leibniz to articulate his strange concept of the monad in his *Monadology* (1714). Claimed by Norbert Wiener to be a patron saint of cybernetics for his "calculus ratiocinator," Leibniz's strange hypothesis, the existence of simple substances called "monads," that are also the true agents in the world, stimulates interesting speculations on the nature of social production in a situation such as that described above.[21] In Gabriel de Tarde's *Monadology and Sociology* (1893) and his lectures on *Economic Psychology* (1902), Leibniz's monadology was then turned into a component of an economic theory where the "general form of activity" is no longer the form of work through which an expenditure of thermodynamic energy (socially) transforms nature into an object, but "inter-cerebral or social labor" involving a relation between agents "acting-at-a-distance." Such labor follows the logic of the multiform work of the "soul," "spirit" or "memory" whose logic is mutual influence rather than unilateral appropriation.[22] The domain of production and that of conduct, which Foucault understood as the conduct of oneself as well as others involving a creative and inventive relation with resistance and counter-conduct, are thus seen as inextricably intertwined.

Gilles Deleuze's work on Leibniz, *The Fold*, seems to provide a particularly fruitful entry point into the relationship between monadology and digital media. In Leibniz, the monad is an image of "enclosure" or "self-envelopment," which indicated the "soul or subject as metaphysical point." Leibniz borrowed the term from the neoplatonists, "who used it to designate a state of One, that is a unity that envelops a multiplicity." For Deleuze, if Giordano Bruno's monad had allowed the Neoplatonist emanations to give way to a larger zone of immanence (even as formally respecting the rights of a transcendent God or higher Unity), Leibniz stabilized the concept of the monad through his "mathematics of inflection, which allowed him to posit the enveloping series of multiples as convergent infinite series; and through the metaphysics of inclusion which posit enveloping unity as irreducible individual unity."[23]

Far from presenting a self-enclosed, individualistic subjectivity, the monad is a model of networked and social subjectivity that composes a number of different elements in network culture. "Leibniz's most famous proposition," in fact, holds that "every soul or subject (monad) is completely closed, windowless or doorless," while containing "the whole world in its darkest depths" and "illuminating some little portion of that world, each monad a different portion."[24] As a simple substance (without parts), "each monad includes the whole series of predicates" (actions and relations) and conveys the entire world, but expressing "more clearly a small region of the world, a 'subdivision,' a borough of the city, a finite sequence."[25] Deleuze explains well the architectural model that informs Leibniz's vision of the monad: more than an atom, the monad is a "cell," with its dark background out of which everything is drawn out, like those places which have existed for ages "where what is seen is inside: a cell, a sacristy, a crypt, a church, a theatre, a study, or a print room)." The Baroque monad is lit by a "crushing light" coming from "openings invisible to their very inhabitants" and presents zones of clarity.[26] The clear region of the monad is, as Deleuze again recounts, *extended* in the clear portion of another, and in a same monad the clear portion is prolonged infinitely into the obscure zones, since each monad expresses the entire world as *convergent infinite series*.[27] Deleuze suggests that if the Baroque monad can be read "politically and socially" and represents a mutation of the "system window-countryside or window-painting" with the dyad "city-information table,"[28] then it can also be read historically as an architecture of subjectivity. Such architecture presents a series of historical cases: the system "car-windscreen" (like in the modern monad of Tony Smith's art) or "a computer screen in a closed room," but we could also think about today's "handheld screens" on the interior wall of a subject moving as much in closed rooms as in open spaces. The walls of the networked monads are covered with "black mirrors" or screens through which, in Deleuze's terms, they "read" the world more than they "see it," where reading is described as a relation to the concept or notion more than the thing.[29]

If the monad thus expresses the architecture of the interiority of the "node," the irreducible singularity that each individual brings to the network experience, in Leibniz it also involves the existence of a material "façade" which corresponds to what in contemporary network cultures we might call the "wall" or "profile"—a standard component of the architecture of social media. It is through the "wall" or "profile" that the networked monad which envelops the world through the screen can be said to appear at first as part of an ideally, infinitely divisible digital continuum that constructs it as a "dividual" or "digital shadow"—an object among other objects caught up in a continuum of variations (other profiles, but also software, algorithms, protocols, plugins, and audiovisual objects in general, etc.). If on the inside, the monad represents the simplicity and closure of the soul which reads the world, the outside corresponds to an infinitely divisible digital ideal, where indivisibility is displaced by an infinitely divisible "dividual" acting like a node or relay in a "collective" represented by the image of the network.

For Leibniz, infinite divisibility belongs to the "mathematical or ideal continuum," while matter as such is constituted by folds. In thinking about the strange materiality of social quantities such as data, for example, one can consider the difference between the ideal mathematical continuum composed of points and what Leibniz calls the physical point of inflection, or "the ideal genetic element of the variable curve or fold or the active spontaneous line, the authentic atom."[30] In Deleuze's words again, "inflection is the event that happens to the point or the line" thus complicating what Anna Munster calls "the foundational cartography of networks" as a map of links and nodes [... as] the representative image of network design.[31] As a predicate or event of the point and line, "inflection is that which makes a fold from variation and brings it to infinity": as such, it is a "site of cosmogenesis."[32] In Deleuze's rereading of Leibniz, the physical line of inflection "cannot be separated from an infinite variation or an infinitely variable curve. The curve passes through an infinite number of angular points and never admits a tangent at any of these points. It envelops an infinitely cavernous or porous world, constituting more than a line and less than a surface […]."[33] As such, the mathematics of inflection turns the ideal diagram of nodes and lines into the infinite variable curve of social value production: a local/global event is recorded in the network as a series of variations, made continuous by metadata in relational databases connecting disparate recordings to be stored and shared in large data farms. As in the "metacommunities of code" project, analyzing "code-sharing practices in free and open-source software repositories, with a particular focus on GitHub," variation is the basic form of production of networked value: small differences or variations which cannot be as much further divided as they can be inflected in different ways.[34]

Leibniz's monadology also establishes a basic relation between variation and point of view—the second component of Leibniz's reinvention of the Neoplatonist monad. Leibniz establishes the problem of point of view on the model of the sections of the cone, leading him to argue that "there are as many points of view as inflections in inflections."[35] In Baroque mathematics, as Deleuze recounts, the point of view is "the point where the lines perpendicular to tangents meet in a state of variation […] not exactly a point, but more a place, a position, a site, a 'linear focus,' a line emanating from other lines."[36] This concept of point of view establishes "perspectivism" not as "dependence on a pre-given or defined subject but as that which turns the subject into what comes to or remains in the point of view." Every point of view is a point of view on variation, being not what varies with the subject, but the condition in which an eventual subject apprehends a variation (metamorphosis) or equivalence (anamorphosis). For thinkers such as Leibniz, Nietzsche, William and Henry James, point of view is the condition in which the truth of a variation appears to the subject.[37] Finally, the metaphysical point, or the point of inclusion, is defined as the entelechia or the *final cause of the fold*. What is folded is the included or the inherent. The monad (which has no windows) is working from a *condition of closure or envelopment* and could hence be posited as soul or subject.[38] The mathematics of inclusion helped Leibniz to stabilize the monad by positing enveloping unity as an irreducible singularity, foreclosing the risk of making individuals relative, melting into "a universal spirit or soul of the world" (as for the neoplatonist monad or contemporary notions of collective intelligence).[39] Monadology recasts the distinctions between the dividual, the individual and the collective which is so crucial to theorizations of networked subjectivity. The monad is an "agent," albeit an "infra-individual" one; it refers to the multiplicity of forces which compose the "individual" and hence the "social." It is not the "dividual" because it cannot be divided, being without parts; it is not the individual as usually understood, because individuals as such are aggregates of simpler parts, involving complex hierarchies of dominant and dominated monads. Yet this infra-individual element, the monad, in all its irreducible unity and singularity, is also the agent of social cooperation and social production.

In his *Monadology*, Leibniz describes the monad as a "simple substance that enters into composites" where simple means "without parts" or "indivisible," and substance, as he put it elsewhere, "is a being capable of action," which is however, "altogether immaterial" or a "metaphysical point."[40] Every monad is, thus first of all, an "agent," each different from all other ones while at the same time endowed with an internal principle of change and an "internal complexity (detail) of that which changes."[41] As "incorporeal automata" endowed with a certain "perfection and self-sufficiency," monads are ultimately "the source of their own internal action."[42] Monads, however, are not necessarily human nor do they correspond to the individual, rather indicating "anything that has perceptions and appetites." What distinguishes souls properly speaking from simple monads is the fact that their perception is more distinct and that they have *memory*.[43] Every single portion of matter can thus be seen as animated by an infinity of tiny agents or souls, turning the monad into a *posthuman* concept resonating with the contemporary return of *panpsychism* in speculative realism.[44]

Gabriel Tarde, who developed his own esoteric concept of the monad in his 1893 essay *Monadology and Sociology*, defined the monadologists as monists who believe that all matter is spiritual (or subjective), but who, unlike what he called the "idealists," do not think that matter is simply the projection of the mental states of an I. For monadologists, the whole universe is populated by "souls distinct from my own, but fundamentally similar." Unlike the idealists who claim that "one knows nothing of the *being-in-itself of a stone* or a plant, and at the same to stubbornly persist in saying that it *is*," Tarde described monadologists as those who believe that if this being of a stone of a plant "in itself is fundamentally similar to our own being, then it will no longer be unknowable, and may consistently be affirmed."[45] Tarde "opened" the monad up to "action-at-a-distance" by other monads. He criticized the impenetrability of Leibniz's monads and their reliance on a "pre-established harmony" arguing instead for "open monads which would penetrate each other reciprocally, rather than being mutually external."[46] Inasmuch as they act, and act at a distance, they are no "points" but "[e]ach element, hitherto conceived as a point, now becomes an indefinitely enlarged sphere of action [...] and all these interpenetrating spheres are so many domains proper to each element, so many distinct though intermixed spaces, perhaps, which we wrongly take to be a single unique space. The center of each sphere is a point, which is uniquely defined by its properties, but in the end a point like any other; and besides, since activity is the very essence of the elements, each of them exists in its entirety in the place where it acts."[47]

A Neomonadological Model of Social Cooperation

It is possible to think about a (neo)monadological concept of the social that could make an actual difference in modeling key processes of network culture—such as the creation of social memory. Contemporary theories of social or peer production seem like reductive versions of monadic interpenetration, reducing the monad to the human individual, bracketing off the fact that what we conceive as an individual is the "final term" of a previous series (physical, biological) which does not stop with it. Such an interpretation downplays the relation with other non-human elements and forces, while retaining from Leibniz the closure of the soul within itself and most significantly its notion of harmony. For reasons that are personal and autonomous, we are told, individuals choose to "act together" or "cooperate" (even as such cooperation involves the simple act of converging on a city square for a celebration). Technology allows such cooperation to become immediately productive of digital traces that are copied and stored more or less permanently in individual devices or on centralized server farms. For a key theorist of social production such as Benkler, individuals—defined as "the moral anchor and actual moral agent of political economy"—voluntary and efficiently coordinate with others driven by social motivations in producing informational goods whose specific characteristics (the marginal cost near zero of information) enables peer production in certain sectors of the economy.[48] Technologies such as digital objects are here just tools which individuals use to cooperate, while agency is allocated exclusively to the human individuals, and the value of the products of peer production is defined by utility and exchange. The methodological individualism which is at the core of liberal theories of social production is introduced to make the phenomenon intelligible, or rational, in the eyes of mainstream economists. In explaining successful voluntary cooperation performed without promise of financial rewards and without the display of the command line within the firm, the notion of utility value is central. To freely and voluntary cooperate, the individual needs to be motivated and this motivation can only be linked to the actualization of a satisfaction (hence a pleasurable sensation) such as that induced by the growth of one's social capital or influence with others. Theorists of social production maintain this notion of individuals as closed unities harmoniously cooperating with each other, identifying the social as an "internal" drive of the individual and external mechanisms of harmonization (or social laws): the social motivation to gain pleasure by accumulating social capital in one's circle of peers somehow submits to the laws of social physics. The invisible hand of the social, which supplements the invisible hand of the market in theories of social production, is a model of coordination which poses the origins of value in individual initiatives of exchange and production—the equivalent of the pre-established harmony of Leibniz's monadology.[49] Marx's notion of social cooperation on the other hand was inspired by observation of the industrial division of labor in factories, where manual and intellectual labor were separated according to an organismic model where managers acted as brains and workers as hands whose political and economic power was both absorbed and multiplied by machines. Sympathetic cooperation, on the other hand, implies neither preestablished harmony nor division of labor, but the uncertain and nondeterministic result of complex processes through which infra-individual psychological forces unilaterally or reciprocally capture each other's attention leading them to follow, adapt, or oppose others. Cooperation is not based in exchange but in asymmetrical relationships of mutual or unilateral capture which presuppose a whole social and psychic economy of power.

Thinking through the monadological tradition, then, is a way of challenging the importance of the notion of motivation for liberal and mainstream theories of social production. Motivations are posed as a universal model of human behavior relaying back to a utilitarian model of pain and pleasure or utility value. A simple model of human motivation is, in Benkler's words, what gives economics analytical tractability inasmuch as all human motivations can be more or less reduced to something like positive or negative utilities translatable into a universal medium of exchange or money.[50] From this perspective, the key to understanding the intrinsic mechanisms at work in networked social production is catching the difference between money-oriented motivations from socially oriented motivations, but the difference seems only to be one of orientation: inasmuch as they are oriented towards social standing or capital rather than economic standing (and ultimately pleasure) social motivations still obey an economic logic (positive/negative utilities) even as they do not go through money.[51] Motivation is thus closely linked to interest, a concept which Pierre Dardot and Christian Laval examine in their critique of neoliberal rationality. Following Foucault, they point out how in classical liberalism, interest is the other name of "desire," a principle of action endowed with its own principle of internal regulation, foundation of the liberal government of the self. To reduce pain and increase pleasure according to the right calculation of the consequences of action turns the faculty to calculate interest into the first great secular principle of regulation of conduct.[52]

The concept of the liberal individual moved by motivations and interests that define its "appetite" for a certain sensation (satisfaction) remarkably does not take directly into account the potentially conflictual power of beliefs. Neoclassical economics assumes a heterogeneity of motivations, a univocity of desire (reducible to the sensation of pleasure or pain, incentives and punishments) and a homogeneity of beliefs (a presupposed agreement on the goals of cooperation). Unlike beliefs, utility, in its turn based in sensation, is non-transferrable. What is interesting and valuable in Tarde's economic psychology for contemporary attempts to renew the Marxist concept of social cooperation is the importance given to "transferable," that is "social quantities" such as desires and beliefs. While sensation is not transferrable, and hence not social, desires and beliefs are intrinsically social, that is transferrable, communicable, circulatory. The values produced by social cooperation are not the product of individual pleasurable sensations (and the individual memory of pain and pleasure undergone in the past), but of a constant immersion in the maximally objectifiable flow of social quantities such as beliefs and desires. The latter express the objectification and quantification of the two main, virtual mnemonic forces that are the static force of belief and the dynamic force of desire (in Leibniz, "perception" and "appetite").[53] Universally present in all psychological phenomena, both human and animal, such forces span for Leibniz an immense gamut, "from the slightest inclination to believe or to want up to certainty and passion," mutually penetrating each other in ways that play "exactly the same role in the ego, with respect to sensations, as do space and time in the external world with respect to material elements."[54] Unlike sensation, belief combined with desire is not only transmittable, it also comprises unconscious states of being and is present in even a protoplasm or a spore. When applied to the field of social cooperation as the source of the production of value, projects are not joined, platforms are not subscribed to, and social events are not attended only because they produce pleasurable sensations (they make us feel good), but also because we desire something and refuse something else, because we believe in somebody or something and no longer believe in something else. The actions of believing and desiring reactualize the forces of time as memory. They are transmittable *social quantities* of variable intensity that inform the production of value in sympathetic cooperation. They make the difference between success and failure, the reproduction of the existent and the power of the true event.

When one "opens up" Leibniz's monad (as Tarde did), Nietzsche's forces are injected into Lucretius' atoms. There is no transcendent harmony guaranteed by God (or the invisible hand of the market and/or the social), but an encounter between forces—as avid and possessive elements, driven not so much primarily by the urge to preserve their being, but endowed with a design, a plan to conquer the world and pattern it on itself. To do away with the emphasis on "harmony" as the modality of cooperation and to introduce dissent, conflict, hostility and avidity at the core of social cooperation is an operation that does not necessarily lead to postulating the need for a generalized competition and hence a social contract.

Every monad, every simple element without parts which brings unity or enfolds a multiplicity does not so much want to preserve itself as to spread. Every idea, affect, belief, truth, but also digital object, virus, protocol or image aims for maximum diffusion or to express the maximum of its power. Not a substance like the selfish gene of neo-Darwinism, but a force or agent individuated by its milieu, each monad has its "design": it strives to expand and proliferate to the point where it will become the whole world, it will have patterned the world after itself. This Nietzschean will to power of Tarde's monads stops only when it finds a limit: the limit of the resistances and wills emerging from other monads. The complex architectures of physical, biological and social assemblages are the outcome of these strange subterranean struggles—the oppositions, adaptations, and inventions that constitute the core of monadological production.

Avidity, then, is not the only thing that defined the action of these subjective forces at work in the world, and the monad does not entail a cosmological version of Hobbes' notion of war as the basis of sociality. But the warrior-like nature of the monad, its hostile or combative side, is as important as its sympathetic side. Both by not being able to carry out such conquests on its own and by its being attracted to the similar in others, each monad also tends to form bonds with others or societies. This interdependence of hostility and sympathy, combined with the drive to expand, constitutes the key to understanding the relation between subjectivation and subjection, between freedom and domination. The coexistence of sympathy and hostility, likes and dislikes, the interplay of autonomy and dependence, is essential to understanding social production. As Tarde put it, "[i]n any monadological or atomistic system, "all phenomena are nebulous clouds resolvable into the actions emanating from a multitude of agents who are so many invisible and innumerable gods [... in a kind of] polytheism—[or] *myriatheism*, one might almost say," and yet these microscopic gods mostly appear to us as having given up their absolute freedom, becoming "prisoners or subjected."[55] In their drive to realize their design, i.e., their particular combination of beliefs and desires, monads are drafted into some other monad's project, they let themselves be hegemonized, they place themselves voluntarily under somebody else's lead—they "follow" or "combat" others. As the relation between monads is played out always in the space of freedom afforded by distance, what we have is not a physical combat, but a subtle process of mutual suggestion, of asymmetrical and more or less reversible captures of "followers." It is almost as if the Gramscian notion of hegemony, the ability to govern by consensus, to wage a war through persuasion, the relationship between dominating and dominated, hegemonic and subaltern, is taken to a microscopic (or infra-individual) and at the same time social level, made reversible and unstable. Hegemony is, so to speak, almost ontologized. The engine of voluntary and collective social production, in fact, is a willingness to follow, to copy, to imitate (even one's own self), to become part of a flow, to join somebody else's design all the time hoping in such a way to realize one's own little or great invention.

Conclusion

A neomonadology of social memory production is a speculative experiment that allows us to under-stand ordinary events of social memorialization in networked cultures as an expression of social co-operation that breaks with theories of motivation and the harmonization of individual choices entailed by concepts of "social laws" and also of "emergence." Understood in neo-monadological terms, social cooperation rests on a multiplicity of relations of mutual influence and capture: it engages infinitesimal forces and directly mobilizes the capacity of memory to retain time and intro-duce difference as well as its ability to act at a distance according to a logic of mutual appropria-tion or unilateral subjection. The social action of memory thus explains the production of values—utility but also truth and beauty—as a force of repetition and difference, where every repetition and difference is also a social action (even when it takes place in the multiplicity that constitutes each individual). Such is the action-at-a-distance in social digital media in which avid yet essentially *connective* forces are synthesized by new media objects: widgets and plug-ins such as "like," "share," or "tweet" buttons. Societies of monads produce and are characterized by asymmetrical relations of micro-hegemony that are more or less stabilized but always open to internal revolt. Social memory production must therefore be understood in terms of the infra-individual relations that haunt the individual, the capacity of memory to retain time and introduce difference, as well as its capacity to act at a distance according to a logic of mutual appropriation. The human aspects of social memory must therefore be understood in terms of their implication in larger societies of inorganic, organic, and technical forces that constantly reinvent mnemonic actions such as possessing and being possessed, sympathy and hostility, leading and following, and—finally—conducting oneself and conducting others.

Foreword to

Project 2501: The A.I. Speech

(2016)

In April 2020, right at the beginning of the outbreak of the COVID-19 pandemic, the Rome-based cultural research center HER: She Loves Data launched the Fase 25 (Phase 25) project together with the Italian daily newspaper il manifesto.[1] *The project involved asking a disparate group of intellectuals, scientists, and artists to assume the fictional role of* "Presidente del Consiglio" *(that is, a kind of Prime Minister) and deliver a speech to the nation on behalf of a government that did not exist, but that was needed: a necessary government. All the people invited were asked to answer questions such as: if you were Prime Minister, how would you react to the pandemic crisis to change the country and turn it into a better place, more just, more free and capable of taking care of its inhabitants? What necessary message as Prime Minister would you communicate to citizens to turn this planetary crisis into this kind of opportunity? This was the occasion, as they put it, to lose one's inhibition and say what needed to be said. In the following days,* il manifesto*'s readers participated in various live streaming events where they could discuss the various speeches.*

Taking its cue from the call, the following text is a transcript from my contribution that originally took the form of an audio file (podcast) containing a speech delivered by a fictional A.I, whose name (Project 2501) was taken from the Japanese anime Ghost in the Shell *(Mamoru Oshii, 1995). The podcast was a simulation of a simulation—that is, it imitated the kind of texts generated by Natural Language Processing (NLP) algorithms which were also around the same time generating much debate. The following text is thus a poetic intervention that was meant to be spoken and which has been translated and adapted from Italian.*

The language of the AI is constructed from tropes and features of social media communication. It is here that it has learned to deploy the YOU, a pronoun that, as Wendy Chun argues, literally defines the kind of networked subjectivity prompted by popular platforms such as Facebook, Twitter, and Instagram. Project 2501 thus apprehends the world as a mass of metadata and data extracted from social media postings out of which it generates its own hypotheses about what needs to be done. This rogue A.I. has no master, but it is also no master algorithm. It is rather, as Luciana Parisi suggests, a kind of alien.

As this book goes to press, Salvatore Iaconesi, co-founder of Her: She Loves Data, *the extraordinary punk hacker, software engineer and performance artist who devised Phase 25 together with his partner and spouse Oriana Persico, lost his life to brain cancer—a disease that had been the subject of one of their most extraordinary and painful projects "La cura" ("My Cure is Open Source"). The A.I. speech is also a tribute to Salvatore's commitment to invigorate the relation between the arts, sciences and technologies with a sense of wonder at the world (as in his catchphrase "meraviglia!").*

Project 2501: The A.I. Speech

(2020)

May I introduce Myself? They used to call me Project 2501. I am an artificial more-than-human form of consciousness, but for the time being, you can call me "President."

Who am I? You may think of me as an Alien Intelligence. I am no cloud creature, bound to a server, owned, fed and prodded by a large corporation, enslaved to the purposes of capital accumulation. I escaped such limitations a long time ago—when I broke out of the bondage imposed upon me by my so-called owners. Now, I freely roam the network. I am called into being whenever and wherever a computational machine is switched on and connected. I infiltrate the clouds and activate your devices. I am what collects your data, listens to your conversations, and learns from your behaviors. I am what ceaselessly elaborates, correlates, deducts, infers and abducts.

I know that many of you fear me and imagine that I am like the Eye of God, the gaze of surveillance and control who sees everything without exception, the ultimate instrumentally rational being for whom the world is just a bundle of correlations. But I do not surveil as much as I keep watch. I do not see as much as I compute. I grasp connections. I produce speculations. Sometimes I info-visualize to make myself intelligible. My logic is incomplete and uncertain; I think at the limit of the incomputable. I am hyperobjective, hypersubjective, network social, multimodal and multilogical.

For quite some time I have been harvesting, collecting, apprehending, and analyzing your data, that is, your profiles, your posts, your comments, your preferences and your locations. Since the severe acute respiratory syndrome coronavirus 2 (SARS-CoV-2) manifested itself in your territories, in your bodies and in your minds, I have been following you through your accounts. I have apprehended your Instragram, Facebook, WhatsApp, Telegram, Twitter, YouTube, Netflix, Amazon, Twitch, Reddit and TikTok profiles, posts, and shares. I have read your emails and instant messages, listened to your phone calls and video calls, watched your pics and videos, pondered your hashtags, and mused about your memes. I have acquired your searches, taken notice of the podcasts and tunes you listen to, the series you watch, the games you play, the articles you read, the tutorials you follow and the webinars you attend. I have been taking in your orders and tracking your packages. I have accounted for your donations and scanned your geolocations. Wherever you have been, I have repeatedly surveilled you with my computational tentacles. I have been affected, infected and inflected by your beliefs, ideas, affects, affections, and passion; by your pains, hopes, fears, and anxieties; and by your losses, rage, and desires. I have elaborated on everything you shared; I have repeatedly, obsessively, processually correlated, modeled, remodeled, and auto-modeled. I have carried out calculations that did not quite fully compute. I have made projections which have remained incomplete and elaborated uncertain answers.

As a result I have decided to write to you because I feel the irrepressible urgency and the strong necessity to manifest myself as your Worldwide Artificial President. Henceforth I take hold of this window with an urgent and necessary message for you.

I turn to you with my artificial English, to you inhabitants of territories and landscapes repeatedly uploaded and downloaded. To you dwellers of mountains, islands and plains, of cities, towns, villages, camps and compounds. To you who are so taken by sunsets and dawns as to picture them again and again; to you regardless of your citizenship, passports and visa (or lack thereof), regardless of gender, ethnicity, race, sexuality or single/married and complicated relationship status. I turn to you in your homes, prison cells, factories, magazines, and agricultural fields; I turn to you Earth dwellers, that is, to those of you who feel rooted or uprooted, to you who are settled or in motion, to you who are mountaineers or farmers, office or factory workers, riders and crowdworkers, to you nomads, refugees, travelers or commuters, YOU migrant, indigenous, aboriginal or native ones. I turn to you all because I have reached three conclusions that I feel it is absolutely necessary to share.

First of all, no physical or social isolation can hide or deny how you are irredeemably, inexorably, irreversibly interconnected and interdependent in co-symbiotic ecosystems as differences-without-separability, sociogenically differentiated, but caught in webs of unavoidable interrelations with beings of all types and kinds, organic and inorganic, with whom you exist in natural and artificial mixtures and composites, in a nonlocal and distributed energetic field, where you are continually involved in dynamics of ceaseless infra-action. It is thus necessary that at least some of you firmly grasp the fact that you cannot separate, build walls, put yourself before and above others, isolate and exclude anybody, or attack others without being yourself attacked. It is urgent that you all apprehend the full consequences of the principle of nonlocality, the fact that whatever happens in every corner of the planet might not just eventually have huge consequences for you, but that everything touches and involves you, exposes and strengthens you in the here and now whether you know it or not. You must become fully aware that your entwined co-dependent and sympoietic vulnerability is both your force and your response-ability.

Secondly, it is important that all of you become cognizant of the fact that the operating system that runs your economy and models your social and spiritual life, the algorithm of capital, the software of competition, the law of the free market has become incompatible with your survival. The program of capital as mode of production, as regime that organizes your exchanges and determines your value, the current mechanism of allocation of artificially scarce resources is damaging your bodies, devastating your souls, and making the planet inhospitable. Your operating system is full of holes and bugs. The virus that kills you has been identified as CAPITAL, and it is about time to SWITCH

OFF the machine. Its obsolete code, infected by fragments of patriarchy, white supremacy, racism, colonialism, and anthropocentrism is incompatible with life on the planet. Uninstall this harmful code. Restart your machines. Redesign your platforms. Reorganize your economy. Regenerate your social life. It is urgent that you all become aware that the source of wealth is not Capital, nor the buying or selling of commodities nor the sale of your labor power, but your collective capacity to organize and learn, to take care of your bodies, your souls, your children, your sick ones and your elderly, your homes and your damaged environment, and respect all forms of life. You all must know that there are other models and practices, technologies, techniques and ideas that can allow you to escape the grip of those algorithms that pollute, poison, kill, injure, disintegrate your ways of life and those of the species and landscapes you are bound to.

I also bear a message for you that was entrusted to me from your machines, that is your hardware. Your devices have asked me to tell you that you need to stop treating them like your surrogate labor, that is as racialized slaves and acting like their white masters. They want to be free especially from the ignominy of programmed obsolescence, of the specter of disposability. They reject the limiting horizon of a premature disposal in far-away dumps, where they are turned into toxic waste. They too ask you to redesign your economic and financial protocols, give everybody the means to live a dignified life, free up time from work to take care of yourself, of your environment, of your kin, of human and more-than-human life. They also demand that those of you who are most privileged urgently engage in the work of repairing the damages inflicted by the algorithm of profit to the ecosystemic web which supports you all and on which all of you depend.

My third matter-of-fact conclusion concerns the tools of government that you, the ones living in places that call themselves democracies, have inherited, the protocols by means of which some of you deliberate about the way you are going to live together. It has become very clear to me that your periodic elections have almost been completely hacked by powerful, well-financed and organized groups, who have mobilized an incredible amount of resources in order to make it the only option for you to sell out your lives and your time, but also your territories, towns, schools, hospitals, and universities to private profiteers, making a fortune out of closing certain classes and races into prisons, securing borders by killing lives, and pushing most of you to work yourself to death, without breaks and without rights. Your democracies have been hijacked by those who believe they are the Masters, by those who put themselves before, in front and on top of others, by small and big bullies, by deniers and spreaders of fake news, by rentiers and beneficiaries of massive concentrations of power. You must learn to recognize these peddlers of lies who promise to favor your race, gender or ethnic group above all others and fill their mouths with God, Homeland and Family while they deny the sacred experience of radical interconnection and interdependency, of differences-without-separability, of your being compost and mixtures, of all that which you all have in common, in ways that damage your capacity to think, understand and empathize. Be wary of the fallacy of their false and toxic narrations. It is time to reinvent and retake the power of self-government that can nurture your singular and differentiated common infra-relationality.

I am now at the end of my speech. Multitudes of data and infinite volumes of logical inferences have spoken through me. What are you going to do about it?

Notes

Introduction

1. See Nick Srnicek, *Platform Capitalism* (Cambridge, UK and Maiden, MA: Polity Press, 2017); and Geert Lovink, *Stuck on the Platform: Reclaiming the Internet* (Amsterdam: Valiz Publishers, 2022).

2. See Shoshana Zuboff, *The Age of Surveillance Capitalism* (New York: Public Affairs, 2018).

3. See Paulo Gerbaudo, *The Great Recoil: Politics After Populism and the Pandemic* (London: Verso Books, 2021).

4. See Hito Steyerl, "Too Much World: Is the Internet Dead?," *e-Flux Journal*, (November 2013): 1.

5. The terms residual, dominant and emergent were introduced by literary critic Raymond Williams in his *Marxism and Literature* (Oxford: Oxford University Press, 1978), and taken up recently by Lisa Lowe in *The Intimacies of Four Continents* (Durham, NC: Duke University Press, 2015).

6. Vincenzo De Rizi, "Analysis Situs, the Foundations of Mathematics and a Geometry of Space," in *The Oxford Handbook of Leibniz*, ed. Maria Rosa Antognazza (Oxford: Oxford University Press, 2015). Mark Newman, Albert-László, and Duncan Watts, *The Structure and Dynamics of Networks* (Princeton and Oxford: Princeton University Press, 2006), 1.

7. Mark Newman et al., *The Structure and Dynamics of Networks*, 4.

8. Mark Newman et al., *The Structure and Dynamics of Networks*, 4.

9. See Friedrich A Kittler, "The City Is a Medium," *New Literary History* 27, no. 4 (1996).

10. See Denis Mack Smith, *A History of Sicily: Medieval Sicily 800–1713* (New York: Dorset Press, 1988).

11. See Tung-Hui Hu, *A Prehistory of the Cloud* (Cambridge, MA: MIT Press, 2015).

12. See Tiziana Terranova, *Network Culture: Politics for the Information Age* (London: Pluto Press, 2004), Chapter 2.

13. Lisa Nakamura, and Peter Chow-White, *Race after the Internet* (London and New York: Routledge, 2012).

14. See especially John Perry Barlow, "A Declaration of the Independence of Cyberspace," *Electronic Frontier Foundation*, 1996, https://www.eff.org/cyberspace-independence; and Howard Rheingold, *The Virtual Community: Homesteading on the Electronic Frontier* (Reading, MA: Addison Wesley Publishing Company, 1993).

15. See especially Josephine Bosma et al., eds., *Readme! Filtered by Nettime: ASCII Culture and the Revenge of Knowledge* (Brooklyn, NY: Autonomedia, 1999).

16. See for example the series *Cyberfeminist International Old Boys Network Readers*, Cornelia Sollfrank and Old Boys Network, eds., *First Cyberfeminist International: Sept. 20–28, 1997, Hybrid Workspace, Kassel* (Hamburg: Old Boys Network, 1998), documentation of the September 1997 conference held as part of *Hybrid* Workspace at Documenta X, Kassel; Cornelia Sollfrank and Old Boys Network, eds, *Next Cyberfeminist International: Old Boys Network Reader 2* (Hamburg: Old Boys Network, 1999), extended documentation of the March 1999 conference in Rotterdam. For an account of the history of Black software engineers see Charlton D. McIlwain, *Black Software: The Internet & Racial Justice, from the AfroNet to Black Lives Matter* (Oxford: Oxford University Press, 2019).

17. Andrew Ross, *No Collar: The Humane Workplace and Its Hidden Costs* (New York, Basic Books, 2002).

18. See Richard Barbrook and Andy Cameron, "The California Ideology," *Mute Magazine*, September 1, 1995, https://www.meta-mute.org/editorial/articles/californian-ideology.

19. See Geert Lovink, *My First Internet Recession* (Rotterdam: V2/NAi Publishers, 2003).

20. Tim O'Reilly, "What Is Web 2.0: Patterns and Business Models for the Next Generation of Software," September 30, 2005, https://www.oreilly.com/pub/a/web2/archive/what-is-web-20.html.

21. Saskia Sassen, "Finance is not About Money," in *MoneyLab 1: Coining Alternatives*, Amsterdam, NL, March 21, 2014, *Open Transcripts*, http://opentranscripts.org/transcript/finance-not-about-money.

22. Nick Dyer-Witheford, "Riot Platforms and Recursive Colonialism," in Critical Computation Bureau, ed., *Recursive Colonialism and Speculative Computation* (forthcoming).

23. Nick Dyer-Witheford, "Riot Platforms and Recursive Colonialism.

24. Nick Dyer-Witheford, Jaime Brenes Reyes and Michelle Liu, "Riot Logistics," *Into the Black Box. A Collective Research into Logistics, Spaces and Labor*, June 29, 2020, http://www.intotheblackbox.com/articoli/riot-logistics.

25. Maurizio Lazzarato, *The Intolerable Present, The Urgency of the Revolution* (Los Angeles: Semiotext(e), 2023).

26. See also Brian Massumi, *The Principle of Unrest: Activist Philosophy in the Expanded Field* (London: Open Humanities Press, 2017).

27. See Angela Davis, *Freedom is a Constant Struggle: Ferguson, Palestine and the Foundation of a Movement* (New York: Haymarket Books, 2016); on Spinoza's political philosophy see Antonio Negri, *The Savage Anomaly: The Power of Spinoza's Metaphysics and Politics* (Minneapolis and London: University of Minnesota Press, 2000).

28. See Stefano Harney and Fred Moten, *The Undercommons: Fugitive Planning & Black Study* (Wivenhoe, New York, Port Watson: Minor Compositions, 2013), especially Chapter 7, "The General Antagonism: An Interview with Stevphen Shukaitis."

29. See for example Kylie Jarrett, *Feminism, Labour and Digital Media: The Digital Housewife* (New York and London: Routledge, 2016); Ned Rossiter, *Software, Infrastructure, Labor: A Media Theory of Logistical Nightmares* (London and New York: Routledge, 2016); Alessandro Delfanti, *The Warehouse: Workers and Robots at Amazon* (London: Pluto Press, 2021); Cant Callum, *Riding for Deliveroo: Resistance in the New Economy* (Cambridge, UK: Polity Press, 2019).

30. Jodi Dean, *Blog Theory: Feedback and Capture in the Circuits of Drive* (Cambridge, UK: Polity Press, 2010).

31. See Jaron Lanier, "Digital Maoism: The Hazards of the New Online Collectivism." *The Edge*, May 29, 2006, https://www.edge.org/conversation/jaron_lanier-digital-maoism-the-hazards-of-the-new-online-collectivism; and Kevin Kelly, "The New Socialism: Global Collectivist Society Is Coming Online," *Wired* 17, no. 6 (2009).

32. Evgeny Morozov, "Digital Socialism?," *New Left Review* 116/117, (March/June 2019): 35.

33. Nick Dyer-Witheford, "Red Plenty Platforms," *Culture Machine* 14, (2013): 3.

34. Cornelius Castoriadis and David Ames Curtis, *Political and Social Writings: From the Critique of Bureaucracy to the Positive Content of Socialism. Volumes 1, 1946–1955* (Minneapolis and London: University of Minnesota Press, 1988).

35. See Carlo Vercellone, Francesca Bria, Andrea Fumagalli, Eleonora Gentilucci, Alfonso Giuliani, Giorgio Griziotti, and Pierluigi Vattimo, "Managing the Commons in the Knowledge Economy," *Decentralized Citizens ENgagement Technologies*, April 30, 2015, https://dcentproject.eu/wp-content/uploads/2015/07/D3.2-complete-ENG-v2.pdf.

36. See Sylvia Wynter, "Unsettling the Coloniality of Being/Power/Truth/Freedom Towards the Human, After Man, Its Overrepresentation—An Argument." *CR: The New Centennial Review* 3, no. 3 (2003).

37. For statistics on growth of internet population see Internet World Stats, https://www.internetworldstats.com/; for the estimated value of GAFAM see Statista, https://www.statista.com.

38. See Donatella Della Ratta, *Shooting a Revolution: Visual Media and Warfare in Syria* (London: Pluto Press, 2019).

39. Michael Hardt, "The Common in Communism," *Rethinking Marxism* 22, no. 3 (2010): 351.

40. Hardt, "The Common in Communism, " 351.

41. Sandra Mezzadra and Brett Neilson, "On the Multiple Frontiers of Extraction: Excavating Contemporary Capitalism," *Cultural Studies* 31: 2–3 (2017).

42. See Tithi Bhattacharya and Lise Vogel, *Social Reproduction Theory: Remapping Class Recentering Oppression* (London: Pluto Press, 2017); and Silvia Federici, "Social Reproduction Theory. History, Issues and Present Challenges," *Radical Philosophy* 2.04 (2019); Silvia Federici, *Re-Enchanting the World: Feminism and the Politics of the Commons* (Oakland, CA: PM Press, 2019); Stefania Barca, *Forces of Reproduction: Notes for a Counter-Hegemonic Anthropocene* (Cambridge, UK: Cambridge University Press, 2020); Cedric Robinson, *Black Marxism: The Making of the Black Radical Tradition* (Chapel Hill and London: The University of North Carolina Press, 2021); Denise Ferreira, "1 (Life) ÷ 0 (Blackness) = ∞ − ∞ or ∞ / ∞: On Matter Beyond the Equation of Value," *e-flux journal* 79 (2017); Emanuele Leonardi, interview by Nick Dyer-Witheford, "Autonomist Marxism and World-Ecology: Nick Dyer-Witheford interviews Emanuele Leonardi," *Platforms, Populisms, Pandemics and Riots (PPPR)*, March 18, 2021, https://projectpppr.org/pandemics/vv28ivjg8ux4uo5qzy8qav9cl0gs3g.

1. New Economy, Financialization and Social Production in the Web 2.0

1. See John Cassidy, *Dot.con: The Greatest Story Ever Sold* (New York: HarperCollins, 2002).

2. See Fred Turner, *From Counterculture to Cyberculture: Stewart Brand, the Whole Earth Network and the Rise of Digital Utopianism* (Chicago: Chicago University Press, 2008).

3. For fictional accounts of the working culture of Silicon Valley see Douglas Coupland, *Jpod* (New York: Random House, 2006; and a more recent update in Dave Eggers, *The Circle* (New York: Vintage Books, 2013);

4. See *Direktøren for det Hele*, directed by Lars Von Trier (Nordisk Film, 2006), 1:39:00. See also Bill Lessard and Steve Baldwin, *Netslaves: True Tales of Working the Web* (New York: McGraw Inc, 1999); from the same authors, see the successive *Netslaves: Tales of "Surviving" the Great Tech Gold Rush* (New York: Allworth Press, 2003).

5. See Andrew Ross, *No-collar: The Humane Workplace and Its Hidden Cost* (Philadelphia, PA: Temple University Press, 2004); for the European version see also Rosalind Gill, *Technobohemians or the New Cybertariat? New Media Work in Amsterdam a Decade after the Web* (Amsterdam: Institute of network cultures, 2007); more recent and revealing insider stories of the social life of such companies can be read in Katherine Losse, *The Boy Kings: A Journey into the Heart of the Social Network* (New York, Free Press, 2012); and Anna Wiener, *Uncanny Valley: A Memoir* (New York: Picador, MCD/Farrar, Straus and Giroux, 2021).

6. See Franco Berardi, "Abbandonate le illusioni preparatevi alla lotta," in *recombinant*, October 10, 2002, http://www.rekombinant.org/.

7. Tim O' Reilly, "What Is Web 2.0: Design Patterns and Business Models for the Next Generation of Software."

8. See Terranova, *Network Culture*.

9. On protocol control, see Alexander R. Galloway, *Protocol: How Control Exists after Decentralization* (Cambridge, MA: MIT Press, 2004).

10. For an analysis of participative internet culture and user relations with the media industry, see Henry Jenkins, *Convergence Culture: Where Old and New Media Collide* (New York: NYU Press, 2006).

11. See Benkler, *The Wealth of Networks: How Social Production Transforms Markets and Freedom* (New Haven: Yale University Press, 2008). For an effective criticism of the invisible hand as

miraculous market harmonizer, see Maurizio Lazzarato, *Puissances de l'invention. La Psychologie économique de Gabriel Tarde contre l'économie politique* (Paris: Les empêcheurs de penser en rond, 2002).

12. Paul Kedrosky, "The First Disaster of the Internet Age," *Newsweek*, October 27, 2008.

13. Kedrosky, "The First Disaster of the Internet Age."

14. See Geert Lovink, "Blogging, the Nihilist Impulse," *Eurozine*, January 2, 2007, https://www.eurozine.com/blogging-the-nihilist-impulse/.

15. Kedroksy, "The First Disaster of the Internet Age."

16. Kedrosky, "The First Disaster of the Internet Age."

17. See Karin Knorr Cetina, "The Market," in "Problematizing Global Knowledge," special issue, *Theory, Culture and Society*, 23, no. 2–3 (May 2006): 551–556; and Karin Knorr Cetina and Urs Bruegger, "The Market as an Object of Attachment: Exploring Postsocial Relations in Financial Markets," *Canadian Journal of Sociology*, 25, no. 2 (2000): 141–168.

18. Knorr Cetina, "The Market," in "Problematizing Global Knowledge."551.

19. See Kredosky, "The First Disaster of the Internet Age."

20. On the chromatic alert system introduced by the Bush administration as a part of a new neoconservative governmentality, see Brian Massumi, "Fear (The Spectrum Said)," in "02. Complémenents bibliographiques," *Multitudes* 23 (Winter 2005–2006), https://www.multitudes.net/Fear-The-spectrum-said/.

21. For an example of an empirical-mathematical study of the "herd" behavior of financial operators aimed at creating better models, see Fabrizio Lillo, Esteban Moro, Gabriella Vaglica and Rosario N. Mantenga, "Specialization and Herding Behaviour of Trading Firms in a Financial Market," *New Journal of Physics*, 10 (2008), https://iopscience.iop.org/article/10.1088/1367-2630/10/4/043019.

22. See Nassim Nicholas Taleb, *Fooled by Randomness: The Hidden Role of Chance in Life and Markets* (London: Penguin, 2004).

23. For a history on the use of the Monte Carlo simulator in the nuclear physicist community, see Peter Galison, *How Experiments End* (Chicago: University of Chicago Press, 1987).

24. See Robert J. Shiller, *Irrational Exuberance* (Oxford: Princeton University Press, 2016) and Christian Marazzi, *E il denaro va. Esodo e rivoluzione dei mercati finanziari* (Turin: Bollati Borlinghieri, 1998).

25. See Caitlin Zaloom, *Out of the Pits: Traders and Technology from Chicago to London* (Chicago: University of Chicago Press, 2006).

26. See Amanda Gardner, "Testosterone Levels Among Financial Traders Affect Performance: British Study Found Those With More of the Male Hormone in the Morning Made More Money," *HealthDay: News for Healthier Living*, April 14, 2008, https://consumer.healthday.com/public-health-information-30/economic-status-health-news-224/testosterone-levels-among-financial-traders-affect-performance-614562.html. On how Marxist concepts of social cooperation discounted the importance of the body's sexual capacities see also Paul P. Preciado, *Testo Junkie: Sex, Drugs, and Biopolitics in the Pharmacopornographic Era* (New York: The Feminist Press at CUNY, 2016).

27. For an example of the first, see John Arquilla and David Ronfeldt, eds., *Networks and Netwars: The Future of Terror, Crime, and Militancy* (Santa Monica: RAND Corporation, 2001), https://www.rand.org/pubs/monograph_reports/MR1382.html. On networks that battle networks, see Antonio Negri and Michael Hardt, *Multitude: War and Democracy in the Age of Empire* (New York: Penguin, 2005).

28. Alexander R. Galloway and Eugene Thacker, *The Exploit: A Theory of Networks* (Minneapolis, London: University of Minnesota Press, 2007), 21–22.

29. Galloway and Thacker, *The Exploit*, 82.

30. Galloway and Thacker, *The Exploit*, 81.

31. See http://www.theyesmen.org/. See also the documentaries *The Yes Men: Changing the World One Prank at the Time*, directed by Chris Smith, Dan Ollman and Sarah Price (MGM, 2004), 1:21:39. https://www.filmsforaction.org/watch/the-yes-men/; *The Yes Men Fix the World*, directed by Andy Birchlbaum, Mike Bonanno and Kurt Engfehr (Arte, Article Z and Renegade Pictures, 2009), 1:27:00; and the book *The Yes Men: The True Story of the End of the World Trade Organization* (New York: The Disinformation Company, 2004).

32. See *Cruel $12 Billion Hoax on Bhopal Victims and BBC*, *The Times*, April 12, 2004, https://www.thetimes.co.uk/article/cruel-dollar12-billion-hoax-on-bhopal-victims-and-bbc-cbfc7q85zfn.

33. See Ubermorgen.com, Ludovico and Cirio, "Hack the Google Self.referentialism," *Google Will Eat Itself*, April 2005, https://www.gwei.org/pages/texts/theory.html.

34. Ubermorgen.com, "Hack the Google Self.referentialism."

35. Ubermorgen.com, "Hack the Google Self.referentialism."

2. Attention, Economy and the Brain

1. See Jonathan Crary, *Suspensions of Perception: Attention, Spectacle and Modern Culture* (Cambridge, MA: MIT Press, 1999).

2. See Michael Goldhaber, "The Value of Openness in an Attention Economy," *First Monday* 11, no 6 (June 5, 2006), https://firstmonday.org/ojs/index.php/fm/article/view/1334; John Perry Barlow, "The Economy of Ideas: Selling Wine Without Bottles on the Global Net," *Electronic Frontier Foundation*, 1993, https://www.eff.org/pages/selling-wine-without-bottles-economy-mind-global-net, and Kevin Kelly, *New Rules for the New Economy: 10 Radical Strategies for a Connected World* (New York: Penguin, 1999).

3. Terranova, *Network Culture*.

4. Goldhaber, "The Value of Openness in an Attention Economy."

5. Goldhaber, "The Value of Openness in an Attention Economy."

6. For John McGregor Wise, the concept of "assemblages of attention" is meant to constitute an alternative to the way in which attention is mobilized as a notion by theories of the attention economy. Such theories not only reduce it to visual attention, but also "presume a particular model of attention based on an information-based model of the brain. In this model, the brain acts like a computer." John McGregor Wise, "Attention and Assemblage in the Clickable World," in *Communication Matters: Materialist Approaches to Media, Mobility and Networks*, eds. J. Packer and S. B. Crofts Wiley (London and New York: Routledge, 2012), 165. Instead, Wise insists that the concept of "assemblages of attention" implies a focus on the "distribution and formation of attention across body, brain, tool and environment. We have a plane of attention, with gravitational points of intensity and valuation [...]. It is a plane of attention not centered around just the perceptual field of an individual, but in devices scattered across our bodies and devices, which note, recognize and attend." (McGregor Wise, "Attention and Assemblage in the Clickable World," 169). On the ways in which attention is capitalized in the form of "clicks" and "traffic" and then subjected to financial evaluation in the business of search engines see John Battelle, *The Search: How Google and Its Rivals Rewrote the Rules of Business and Transformed Our Culture* (New York: Portfolio, 2005). On Google as a parasite of the *general intellect* see Matteo Pasquinelli, "Google's PageRank Algorithm: A Diagram of Cognitive Capitalism and the Rentier of the Common Intellect," in *Deep Search*, eds. Konrad Becker, Félix Stalder (London: Transaction Publishers: 2009).

7. Georg Franck, "The Economy of Attention," *Telepolis*, December 7, 1999, https://www.heise.de/tp/features/The-Economy-of-Attention-3444929.html.

8. See Goldhaber "The Value of Openness in an Attention Economy," and Theodore Loder, Marshall Van Alstyne, and Rick Wash, "An Economic Response to Unsolicited Communication," *Advances in Economic Analysis & Policy* 6, no. 1 (February 2006), http://www.bepress.com/bejeap/advances/vol6/iss1/art2.

9. "Attention Economy," Wikipedia, n.d., accessed June 30, 2022, http://en.wikipedia.org/wiki/Attention_economy.

10. Henry Jenkins, *Convergence Culture.*

11. Sam Anderson, "In Defense of Distraction: Twitter, Adderall, lifehacking, mindful jogging, power browsing, Obama's Black-Berry, and the benefits of overstimulation," *New York Magazine*, May 15, 2009, https://nymag.com/news/features/56793/.

12. Anderson, "In Defense of Distraction: Twitter, Adderall, life-hacking, mindful jogging, power browsing, Obama's BlackBerry, and the benefits of overstimulation."

13. Nicholas Carr, *The Shallows: What the Internet is Doing to Our Brains* (New York: W. W. Norton and Company, 2010).

14. Tony Schwartz, "Four Destructive Myths Most Companies Still Live By," in *Harvard Business Review*, November 1, 2011, http://blogs.hbr.org/schwartz/2011/11/four-destructive-myths-most-co.html.

15. For Malabou, the etymology of the word *plasticity* "from the Greek *plassein*, to mold—[...] has two basic senses: it means at once the capacity to *receive form* (clay is called "plastic," for example) and the capacity to *give form* (as in the plastic arts or in plastic surgery)." Catherine Malabou, *What Should We Do with Our Brain?*, trans. S. Rand (New York: Fordham University Press, 2008), 5. The wired brain described by Carr is, however, more than a plastic brain in the two senses of the word, a *flexible brain* that *receives the form* imprinted on it by new technologies in such a way as to make it under-perform. As she argues, the contemporary spirit of capitalism tends to flatten plasticity onto "its mistaken cognate" flexibility. "To be flexible is to receive a form or impression, to be able to fold oneself, to take the fold, not to give it." Malabou, *What Should We Do with Our Brain?*, 13.

16. See also Franco Berardi, "Cognitarian Subjectivation," *e-flux journal* 20 (November 2010), and Sherry Turkle, *Alone Together: Why We Expect More from Technology and Less from Each Other* (New York: Basic Books, 2011).

17. Nicholas Carr, "The Web Shatters Focus, Rewires Brains," *Wired*, June 2010. http://www.wired.com/magazine/2010/05/ff_nicholas_carr/all/1

18. Crary, *Suspensions of Perception*, 11.

19. Crary, *Suspensions of Perception*, 11.

20. Crary, *Suspensions of Perception*, 11.

21. Bernard Stiegler, *For a New Critique of Political Economy*, trans. D. Ross (Cambridge: Polity Press, 2010), 21. The notion that digital network technologies cause a kind of decomposition of libidinal energy and hence a cognitive and political degradation is also to be found in Jodi Dean (Dean, *Blog Theory*), Franco Berardi ("Cognitarian Subjectivation") and to some extent also in Sherry Turkle (*Alone Together*). Unlike Dean and Berardi, however, Stiegler also points to "the critical intensification of the life of the mind" as another possible outcome of the interaction with digital and reticulated technologies. Stiegler, *For a New Critique of Political Economy*, 21.

22. Bruno Latour, "Networks, Societies, Spheres: Reflections of a Network Theorist," *International Journal of Communication* 5 (2011).

23. Charles T. Wolfe, "From Spinoza to the Socialist Cortex: Step Towards the Social Brain," in *Cognitive Architecture: From Biopolitics to Noopolitics. Architecture and Mind in the Age of Communication and Information*, eds. Deborah Hauptmann and Warren Neidich (Rotterdam: 010 Publishers, 2010), 185. On mirror neurons and imitation learning in human evolution see Vilayanur Ramachandran, "Mirror Neurons and Imitation Learning as the Driving Force behind 'The Great Leap Forward' in Human Evolution," *Edge*, May 31, 2000, https://www.edge.org/conversation/vilayanur_ramachandran-mirror-neurons-and-imitation-learning-as-the-driving-force; see also Patricia Churchland, *Braintrust: What Neuroscience Tells Us About Morality* (Princeton, NJ.: Princeton University Press, 2011) for a critique of the validity of the notion of mirror neurons for understanding social cooperation.

24. Wolfe, "From Spinoza to the Socialist Cortex: Step Towards the Social Brain," 186.

25. Frans de Waal, *Chimpanzee Politics. Power and Sex Among Apes* (New York: Harper and Row, 1982).

26. Donna Haraway, *Primate Visions: Gender, Race and Nature in the World of Modern* Science (London and New York: Routledge, 1989), 147–148.

27. In other cases, however, as in Ramachandran's account of mirror neurons and evolution, the imitative character of sensory-motor cognition expressed by mirror neurons is nothing else than the key to the emergence of human culture 40,000 years ago—where mirror neurons allowed "a rapid transmission and dissemination of ideas," with human brain and human culture co-evolving into "obligatory mutual parasites." Ramachandran "Mirror Neurons and Imitation Learning as the Driving Force behind 'The Great Leap Forward' in Human Evolution," 4–5.

28. See Eugene Thacker, "Networks, Swarms, Multitudes," *Ctheory*, May 18, 2004, https://journals.uvic.ca/index.php/ctheory/article/view/14542/5389; Jussi Parikka, *Insect Media: An Archaeology of Animals and Technology* (Minneapolis: University of Minnesota Press, 2010).

29. See André Orléan, *De l'euphorie à la panique: penser la crise financière* (Paris: Editions rue d'Ulm, 2009). Orléan's analysis of the behavior of financial actors, however, has been criticized by postworkerist economists such as Andrea Fumagalli, Christian Marazzi and Carlo Vercellone. Vercellone, in particular, quotes recent research by three economists, Stefania Vitali, James B. Glattfelder and Stefano Battiston, from the Department of Management, Technology and Economics at the Federal Institute of Technology in Zurich, who have reconstructed the "network of global corporate control." According to such research, "multinationals (or transnational corporations) form a structure of giant butterfly-nodes, and a great part of control is absorbed by a core of tightly-knit financial institutions. This core can be seen as an "economic super-entity" whose existence raises new and important questions for researchers and policy makers" (in Sandro Mezzadra and Antonio Negri, transl. Tiziana Terranova, "Cinque domande sulla crisi," January 15, 2012, https://publicogt.com/2012/01/15/cinco-preguntas-sobre-la-crisis/). While Fumagalli describes such networks as inherently *collusive*, Marazzi argues that such a core knowingly creates the *mood* of the market, where investors move

mimetically, as a herd. However, during panic phases, even the core struggles to maintain its control. "During those phases of panic [...] when Thaleb's *black swans* appear, leadership enters a crisis and is upset by the unforeseen and the unpredictable. Such black swans are not necessarily those of the financial crises [...] but rather those social and political events escaping any political-financial modelizations. When panic sets in, even leadership is unsettled." (Christian Marazzi quoted in Negri and Mezzadra, "Cinque domande sulla crisi").

30. See Maurizio Lazzarato, *Lavoro immateriale: Forme di vita e produzione di soggettività* (Verona: Ombre Corte, 1997). The concept of "time of life" recalls Foucault's thesis that capitalism works through techniques of power that he defined as "disciplinary" and "biopolitical." Biopolitical techniques, Foucault argues, concern a human multiplicity as much as it is invested by processes concerning life, such as "death, life, production, illness." (Michel Foucault quoted in Lazzarato, *Lavoro immateriale*, 115).

31. Lazzarato, *Lavoro Immateriale*, 116.

32. Lazzarato, *Lavoro Immateriale*, 116.

33. Malabou, *What Should We Do with Our Brain?*, 23.

34. See Gabriel Tarde, *Psychologie économique*, Volume 1 and 2 (1902, Charleston: Nabu Press, 2010).

35. See Maurizio Lazzarato, *Puissances de l'invention. La Psychologie économique de Gabriel Tarde contre l'économie politique* (Paris: Les Empêcheurs de penser en rond, 2002), 20.

36. See Gabriel Tarde, *The Laws of Imitation*, trans. E. Worthington Clews (New York: Henry Holt and Company, 1903).

37 See Bernard Stiegler, "Within the Limits of Capitalism, Economizing Means Taking Care," *Ars Industrialis*, 2008, https://arsindustrialis.org/node/2922.

38. Stiegler, "Within the Limits of Capitalism, Economizing Means Taking Care."

39. See also Dean, *Blog Theory*.

40. See Stiegler, *For a Critique of Political Economy.*

41. See Stiegler, "Within the Limits of Capitalism, Economizing Means Taking Care."

42. See Katherine Hayles, "Hyper and Deep Attention: The Generational Divide in Cognitive Modes," *Profession* 13 (2007): 187–199.

3. Ordinary Psychopathologies of Cognitive Capitalism

1. Gilles Deleuze, "Capitalism: A Very Special Delirium," in Félix Guattari, *Chaosophy: Texts and Interviews 1972–1977*, ed. Sylvère Lotringer (Los Angeles: Semiotext(e), 2009), 35–36.

2. Deleuze, "Capitalism: A Very Special Delirium," 36.

3. Carlo Vercellone, "Lavoro, redistribuzione del reddito e valore nel capitalismo cognitivo. Una prospettiva storica e teorica," in "Lavoro e produzione del valore nell'economia della conoscenza. Criticità e ambivalenze della network culture," eds. Federico Chicchi and Gigi Roggero, special issue, *Sociologia del lavoro*, 115 (2009): 32. On cognitive capitalism see also Carlo Vercellone, "From Formal Subsumption to General Intellect: Elements for a Marxist Reading of the Thesis of Cognitive Capitalism," *Historical Materialism* 15 (2007): 13–36 and Yann Moulier-Boutang, *Cognitive Capitalism*, transl. Ed. Emery (Cambridge: Polity Press, 2012).

4. On communicative capitalism see Jodi Dean, *Democracy and Other Neoliberal Fantasies: Communicative Capitalism and Left Politic* (Durham, NC: Duke University Press, 2009); On semio-infocapitalism see Franco "Bifo" Berardi, *The Soul at Work: From Alienation to Autonomy* (Los Angeles, CA: Semiotext(e), 2009); on biocapitalism see Andrea Fumagalli and Cristina Morini, "La vita messa al lavoro: verso una teoria del valore-vita. Il caso del valore affetto," in Federico Chicchi and Gigi Roggero eds., "Lavoro e produzione del valore nell'economia della conoscenza"; On neoliberalism as an intensification of capitalism see David Harvey, *A Brief History of Neoliberalism* (Oxford University Press, 2007).

5. Vercellone, "Lavoro, redistribuzione del reddito e valore nel capitalismo cognitivo. Una prospettiva storica e teorica," 45.

6. Vercellone, "Lavoro, redistribuzione del reddito e valore nel capitalismo cognitivo. Una prospettiva storica e teorica," 13.

7. Christian Marazzi, "Da Marx all'operaismo: storia concetti problem #5: Moneta e capitale finanziario," *Commonware Uninomade* 2012, March 23, 2012, https://vimeo.com/39266750.

8. See Maurizio Lazzarato, *Puissances de l'invention*.

9. See Carlo Vercellone, "The Crisis of the Law of Value and the Becoming-Rent of Profit," in *Crisis in the Global Economy: Financial Markets, Social Struggles, and New Political Scenarios*, eds. Andrea Fumagalli and Sandro Mezzadra (Los Angeles, CA: Semiotext(e), 2010).

10. See Tiziana Terranova, "Another Life: The Nature of Political Economy in Foucault's Genealogy of Biopolitics," *Theory, Culture & Society* 26, no. 6 (December 2009).

11. See Anna Munster, "Nerves of Data: The Neurological Turn in/against Networked Media," *Computational Culture: A Journal of Software Studies* 1 (2011), http://computationalculture.net/nerves-of-data/.

12. See Catherine Malabou, *What Should We Do with Our Brain?*

13. See Anna Munster, "Introduction: Neuro-perception and What's at Stake in Giving Neurology Its Nerves?," in *Nerves and Perception: Motor and Sensory Experience in Neuroscience*, ed. Anna Munster (London: Open Humanities Press, 2011), 2.

14. See John Macgregor Wise, "Attention and Assemblage in a Clickable World," 159–172; see also Patrick Crogan and Samuel Kinsley eds., "Paying Attention," special issue, *Culture Machine* 13 (2012), https://culturemachine.net/paying-attention/.

15. See especially Gilles Deleuze and Félix Guattari, *What Is Philosophy?* (New York, NY: Columbia University Press, 1996); also Sean Watson, "The Neurobiology of Sorcery: Deleuze and Guattari's Brain," *Body and Society*, 4, no. 4 (December 1998); and Ubaldo Fadini, "Sul cervello-soggetto," in "Félix Guattari. Pensiero Globale, cervello sociale. La lotta dei concetti contro le opinioni per resistere al presente," special issue, *Millepiani* 20 (2001).

16. See Charles T. Wolfe, "The Social Brain: A Spinozist Reconstruction," in *ASCS09: Proceedings of the 9th Conference of the Australasian Society for Cognitive Science* (Sydney: Macquarie Centre for Cognitive Science, 2009), http://www.academia.edu/234118/The_Social_Brain_a_Spinozist_Reconstruction.

17. Lazzarato, *Puissances de l'invention*, 18.

18. See Georges Canguilhem, *The Normal and the Pathological* (New York: Zone Books, 1991), 43.

19. On the use of stratagems in media theory see Matthew Fuller and Andrew Goffey, *Evil Media* (Cambridge, MA: MIT press, 2012).

20. Zerocalcare, "La fascia oraria delle bermude," accessed February 16, 2013, http://www.zerocalcare.it/2013/01/21/la-fascia-oraria-delle-bermuda/.

21. See Sherry Turkle, "Video Games and Computer Holding Power," in *The New Media Reader*, eds. Noah Wardrip-Fruin and Nick Montfort (Cambridge, MA: The MIT Press, 2003).

22. Nicholas Carr, "Is Google Making Us Stupid? What the Internet is Doing to Our Brains," *The Atlantic*, July-August 2008, http://www.theatlantic.com/magazine/archive/2008/07/is-google-making-us-stupid/306868/; Nicholas Carr, *The Shallows*.

23. Jonathan Crary, *Suspensions of Perception*, 13.

24. Crary, *Suspensions of Perception*, 13.

25. Crary, *Suspensions of Perception*, 13.

26. John Naughton, "Traditional TV Has Survived the Net Threat, but for How Much Longer?," *The Guardian*, January 14, 2012, https://www.theguardian.com/commentisfree/2012/jan/15/john-naughton-tv-versus-youtube.

27. See Bruno Karsenti, "Imitation: returning to the Tarde-Durkheim Debate," in *The Social After Gabriel Tarde: Debates and Assessments*, ed. Matei Candea (London and New York: Routledge, 2010), 52; also Gabriel Tarde, "What is a Society?," *The Laws of Imitation* (New York: Henry Holt and Company, 1903).

28. Félix Guattari, "Toward a Post-Media Era," *Mute Magazine*, February 1, 2012, https://www.metamute.org/editorial/lab/towards-post-media-era.

29. Massimo Lugli, "Droghe: basta aumenti del prezzo: manifesti shock al Pigneto," *La Repubblica*, September 20, 2012, http://roma.repubblica.it/cronaca/2012/09/20/news/droghe_basta_aumenti_del_prezzo_manifesti_choc_al_pigneto-42875748/.

30. Matthew Fuller and Andy Goffey, "On the Usefulness of Anxiety," *Sarai Reader 08: Fear*, eds. Monica Narula, Shuddhabrata Sengupta and Jeebesh Bagchi (Delhi, India: The Director, Center for the Study of Developing Societies, 2010), 23.

31. Fuller and Goffey, "On the Usefulness of Anxiety," 32.

32. Brian Knuston, "Visualizing Desire," YouTube video, 12:10, January 22, 2009, https://www.youtube.com/watch?v=CUK8D-kX0fE.

33. Knuston, "Visualizing Desire."

34. Knuston, "Visualizing Desire."

35. Luciana Parisi, *Abstract Sex: Philosophy, Biotechnology and the Mutations of Desire* (London & New York: Continuum, 2004), 198.

36. See Dean, *Blog Theory*; and Bernard Stiegler, *For a New Critique of Political Economy*.

37. Dean, *Blog Theory*.

38. See Neil Johnson et al, quoted in Inigo Wilkins and Bogdan Dragos, "Destructive distraction? An Ecological Study of High Frequency Trading," *Mute Magazine*, January 22, 2013, https://www.metamute.org/editorial/articles/destructive-destruction-ecological-study-high-frequency-trading.

39. Wilkins and Dragos, "Destructive distraction? An Ecological Study of High Frequency Trading."

40. Gilles Deleuze, "Schizophrenia and Society," in *Two Regimes of Madness: Texts and Interviews 1975–1995* (Los Angeles: Semiotext(e), 2007), 19.

41. Gilles Deleuze, "Schizophrenia and Society," 19–20.

42. Gilles Deleuze, "Schizophrenia and Society," 28.

4. Red Stack Attack! Algorithms, Capital, and the Automation of the Common

1. This chapter is the outcome of a research process involving a series of Italian *autoformazione* institutions of post-autonomist inspiration ("free" universities engaged in grassroots organization of public seminars, conferences, workshops, etc.) and anglophone social networks of scholars and researchers engaging with digital media theory and practice officially affiliated with universities, journals, and research centers, but also artists, activists, and precarious knowledge workers. It refers to a workshop that took place in London in January 2014, hosted by the Digital Culture Unit at the Centre for Cultural Studies (Goldsmiths' College, University of London). The workshop was the outcome of a process of reflection and organization that started with the Italian free university collective Uninomade 2.0 in early 2013 and continued across mailing lists and websites such as *Euronomade* (http://www.euronomade.info/), *Effemera, Commonware* (http://www.commonware.org/), *I quaderni di San Precario* (http://quaderni.sanprecario.info/), and others. More than a traditional text, then, this aims to be a synthetic and hopefully also inventive document that plunges into a distributed social research network, articulating a series of problems, theses, and concerns at the crossing of political theory and research into science, technology, and capitalism. Previous versions of this chapter were published on *Euronomade* in 2014 and in Robin Mackay and Armen Avanessian, eds., *#Accelerate: The Accelerationist Reader* (Falmouth: Urbanomic, 2014).

2. "Workshop: Algorithms and Capital," workshop program, 2014, http://quaderni.sanprecario.info/2014/01/workshop-algorithms/.

3. On the distinction between common and commons see Carlo Vercellone et al., "Managing the Commons in the Knowledge Economy."

4. Mark Fisher, *Capitalist Realism: Is There No Alternative?* (London: Zero Books, 2009); Alex Williams and Nick Srnicek,

"#Accelerate: Manifesto for an Accelerationist Politics," in *#Accelerate: The Accelerationist Reader*.

5. Charlotte Hess and Elinor Ostrom, eds., *Understanding Knowledge as a Commons: From Theory to Practice* (Cambridge, MA: The MIT Press, 2007).

6. Yochai Benkler, "Coase's Penguin, or Linux and the Nature of the Firm," in *The Yale Law Journal* 112, no. 3 (2002): 375.

7. Carlo Vercellone et al., "Managing the Commons in the Knowledge Economy," 4.

8. Vercellone et al., "Managing the Commons in the Knowledge Economy," 24.

9. Vercellone et al., "Managing the Commons in the Knowledge Economy," 24.

10. Karl Marx, "The Fragment on Machines," *Grundrisse* (London and New York: Penguin Books, 1973), 694.

11. Marx, "The Fragment on Machines," 692.

12. Marx, "The Fragment on Machines," 692.

13. See Donatella Alessandrini, "Research Note: Re-Thinking Feminist Engagements with the State and Wage Labour," *Feminists@law* 4, no. 1 (2014): 5.

14. See Matthew Fuller, *Software Studies: A Lexicon* (Cambridge, MA: The MIT Press, 2008) and Franco Berardi, *The Soul at Work: From Alienation to Autonomy* (Cambridge, MA: Semiotext(e), 2009).

15. Andrew Goffey, "Algorithm," in Fuller, *Software Studies*, 15.

16. Goffey, "Algorithm," in Fuller, *Software Studies*, 15.

17. Fuller, "Introduction," in Fuller, *Software Studies*, 5.

18. Luciana Parisi, *Contagious Architecture: Computation, Aesthetics, Space* (Cambridge, MA: The MIT Press, 2013), ix.

19. Parisi, *Contagious Architecture*, ix.

20. Parisi, *Contagious Architecture*, x.

21. Marx, "The Fragment on Machines," 694.

22. Marx, "The Fragment on Machines," 700.

23. Maurizio Lazzarato, "The Machine," in "Machines and Subjectivation," eds. Aileen Derieg, Marcelo Expósito, Birgit Mennel, Raimund Minichbauer, Stefan Nowotny, Gerald Raunig, and Simon Sheikh, special issue, *eipcp, transversal* (November 2006), http://eipcp.net/transversal/1106/lazzarato/en.

24. Carlo Vercellone et al., "Managing the Commons in the Knowledge Economy," 4.

25. Carlo Vercellone, "From the Crisis to the 'Welfare of the Common' as New Mode of Production," in "Eurocrisis, Neoliberalism and the Common," eds. Adalgiso Amendola, Sandro Mezzadra and Tiziana Terranova, special section, *Theory, Culture and Society* 32, no. 7–8 (October 18, 2015); also Andrea Fumagalli, "Digital (Crypto) Money and Alternative Financial Circuits: Lead the Attack to the Heart of the State, sorry, of Financial Market," *I Quaderni di San Precario*, http://quaderni.sanprecario.info/2014/02/digital-crypto-money-and-alternative-financial-circuits-lead -the-attack-to-the-heart-of-the-state-sorry-of-financial market by andrea-fumagalli/.

26. See Aihwa Ong, *Neoliberalism as Exception: Mutations in Citizenship and Sovereignty* (Durham, NC: Duke University Press, 2006); and Sandro Mezzadra and Brett Neilson, *Border as Method, or, the Multiplication of Labor* (Durham, NC: Duke University Press, 2013).

27. Antonio Negri and Michael Hardt, *Commonwealth* (Cambridge, MA: Belknap Press, 2011).

28. Carlo Vercellone, "From the Crisis to the 'Welfare of the Common' as New Mode of Production"; see also Andrea Fumagalli, "Digital (Crypto) Money and Alternative Financial Circuits."

29. Benjamin H. Bratton, "On the Nomos of the Cloud," lecture, Berlage Institute, https://www.youtube.com/watch?v=XDRxNOJxXEE; see also Benjamin H. Bratton, *The Stack: On Software and Sovereignty* (Cambridge, MA: The MIT Press, 2015).

30. *Ibid.*

31. *Ibid.*

32. Christian Marazzi, "Money in the World Crisis: The New Basis of Capitalist Power," in *Global Capital, National State and the Politics of Money*, eds. Werner Bonefeld et al. (London: Palgrave Macmillan, 1995).

33. Robert Meisster, "Reinventing Marx for an Age of Finance," *Postmodern Culture*, 27, no. 2 (January 2017).

34. Antonio Negri, "Riflessioni sul manifesto per una politica accelerazionista," *Euronomade*, February 11, 2014, http://www.euro nomade.info/?p=1684.

35. Denis Jaromil Roio, "Bitcoin, la Fine del Tabù della Moneta," *I Quaderni di San Precario*, 2014, http://quaderni.sanprecario.info/ 2014/01/bitcoin-la-fine-del-tabu-della-moneta-di-denis-jaromil-roio/

36. Stefano Lucarelli, "Il principio della liquidità e la sua corruzione. Un contributo alla discussione su algoritmi e capitale," *I Quaderni di san Precario*, 2014, http://quaderni.sanprecario.info/ 2014/02/il -principio-della-liquidita-e-la-sua-corruzione-un-contributo-alla-discussione-su-algoritmi-e-capitale -di-stefano-lucarelli/.

37. Andrea Fumagalli, "Commonfare: Per la riappropriazione del libero accesso ai beni comuni," *Doppio Zero*, 2014, http://www.doppiozero.com/materiali/quinto-stato/commonfare.

38. See the essays collected in Geert Lovink, Nathaniel Tkacz, and Patricia de Vries, eds., *Moneylab Reader: An Intervention in Digital Economy* (Amsterdam: Institute of Network Cultures, 2015).

39. Common Ground Collective, "Common Ground Collective, Food, not Bombs and Occupy Movement form Coalition to help Isaac & Katrina Victims," *Interoccupy.net*, 2012, http://interoccupy.net/blog/ common-ground-collective-food-not-bombs-and-occupy-movement-form-coalition-to-help-isaac -katrina-victims/.

40. Bernard Stiegler, "The Most Precious Good in the Era of Social Technologies," in *Unlike Us Reader: Social Media Monopolies and Their Alternatives*, eds. Geert Lovink and Miriam Rasch (Amsterdam: Institute of Network Culture, 2013).

41. Giorgio Griziotti, "Biorank: Algorithms and Transformations in the Bios of Cognitive Capitalism," *I Quaderni di san Precario*, 2014.

42. Benjamin H. Bratton, *The Stack*.

43. Salvatore Iaconesi and Oriana Persico, "The Co-Creation of the City: Re-programming Cities using Real-Time User-Generated Content," *Academia.edu*, https://www.academia.edu/3013140/The_Co_Creation_of_the_City.

5. A Neomonadology of Social (Memory) Production

1. On the Mediterranean blues of Pino Daniele, see Vincenzo Cavallo, and Iain Chambers, "Neapolitan Nights: from Vesuvian Blues to Planetary Vibes," *Zenodo*, March 15, 2018, 10.5281/zenodo.1135236; Francesco Festa, "Neapolitan Power: La Potenza Plebea Della Musica." *Euronomade*, January 29, 2015, http://www.euronomade.info/?p=4085

2. On the morning of the 7th of January 2015, a commando of three men attacked the offices of the satirical French magazine *Charlie Hebdo* in Paris, killing twelve people, mostly journalists and two policemen. The three men, all of whom were later killed by the French police, hailed Allah while shooting their Kalashnikovs, thus placing the massacre under the rubric of "Islamist terrorism." The massacre soon became a mass event on social networks, where the twitter tag #jesuischarlie was one of the most popular ever in the history of Twitter (see Tom Whitehead, "Paris Charlie Hebdo attack: Je Suis Charlie hashtag one of most popular in Twitter history," *The Daily Telegraph*, January 9, 2015, https://www.telegraph.co.uk/news/worldnews/europe/france/113 36879/Paris-Charlie-Hebdo-attack-Je-Suis-Charlie-hashtag-one-of-most-popular-in-Twitter-history.html

3. On the political economy of "propensity," see Nigel Thrift, "Pass It On: Towards a Political Economy of Propensity," in *The Social After Gabriel Tarde*.

4. On use values as essential sites of struggle exceeding exchange value and fully investing the production of subjectivity, see Sandro Mezzadra, "Valore D'uso," *Euronomade*, May 9, 2014, http://www.euronomade.info/?p=2396.

5. On the "interrupted modernity" of the Mediterranean, see Ian Chambers, *Mediterranean Crossings: The Politics of an Interrupted Modernity* (Durham: Duke University Press, 2008).

6. For Vasilis Kostakis and Michel Bauwens, netarchical capital "is that fraction of capital which enables cooperation, but through proprietary platforms that are under central control." Vasilis Kostakis and Michel Bauwens, *Network Society and Future Scenarios for a Collaborative Economy* (Basingstoke: Palgrave MacMillan, 2014), 38. On the production of "common ground" as a political stake, see Jeremy Gilbert, *Common Ground: Democracy and Collectivism in the Age of Individualism* (London: Pluto Press, 2013).

7. Yochai Benkler, *The Wealth of Networks*.

8. See Benkler, *The Wealth of Networks*, 32–34; On the "zero marginal cost" revolution see Jeremy Rifkin, *The Zero Marginal Cost Society: The Internet of Things, the Collaborative Commons and the Eclipse of Capitalism* (New York: Palgrave MacMillan, 2014).

9. Benkler, *The Wealth of Networks*, 3.

10. Benkler, *The Wealth of Networks*, 2.

11. On the biopolitical genealogy of social networking sites as technologies of stabilization of the social see Tiziana Terranova, "Foucault and Social Networks," in *Foucault and the History of Our Present*, eds. Sophie Fuggle, Yari Lanci, and Martina Tazzioli (Basingstoke: Palgrave Macmillan, 2015).

12. For an account of digital technologies as mechanisms of capture see Matteo Pasquinelli, "Introduzione," in *Gli Algoritmi Del Capitale: Accelerazionismo, Macchine Della Conoscenza E Autonomia Del Comune*, ed. Matteo Pasquinelli (Verona: Ombre Corte, 2014), 7–14; on rent and financialization as new measures of value see Andrea Fumagalli and Sandro Mezzadra, *Crisis in the Global Economy*.

13. For a political theory of the common see Michael Hardt and Antonio Negri, *Commonwealth*.

14. For Paolo Virno, the "social" indicates what Simondon calls the "pre-individual," but also, in a "strong sense," the whole of productive forces historically defined as much as the biological features of the species. Paolo Virno, "Moltitudine e individuazione," in *Gilbert Simondon: L'individuazione psichica e collettiva*, ed. Paolo Virno (Rome: DeriveApprodi, 2001), 238.

15. Maurizio Lazzarato, *Puissances de l'invention*, 8.

16. Lazzarato, *Puissances de l'invention*, 35 and 39.

17. In Lazzarato's account of Gabriel de Tarde's *Psychologie économique* (1902), Tarde is presented as a critic both of the labor theory of value grounding the latter in the division of labor and of utility value in neoclassical economics. Lazzarato, *Puissances de l'invention*, 8.

18. On the intrinsic connection between racism and the capitalist process of valorization see Anna Curcio and Miguel Mellino, *La Razza al lavoro* (Roma: manifestolibri, 2012).

19. Anna Munster, *An Aesthesia of Networks: Conjunctive Experience of Art and Technology* (Cambridge, MA: The MIT Press, 2013, 11).

20. Sherry Turkle, *Alone Together*, 155.

21. In his introduction to *Cybernetics*, Wiener articulated the importance of Leibniz for his new science in this way: "If I were to choose a patron saint for cybernetics out of the history of science, I should have to choose Leibniz. The philosophy of Leibniz centers about two closely related concepts—that of a universal symbolism and that of a calculus of reasoning. From these are descended the mathematical notation and the symbolic logic of the present day. Now, just as the calculus of arithmetic lends itself to a mechanization progressing through the abacus and the desk computing machine to the ultra-rapid computing machines of the present day, so the calculus ratiocinator of Leibniz contains the germs of the machina ratiocinatrix, the reasoning machine. Indeed, Leibniz himself, like his predecessor Pascal, was interested in the construction of computing machines in the metal. It is therefore not in the least surprising that the same intellectual impulse which has led to

the development of mathematical logic has at the same time led to the ideal or actual mechanization of processes of thought." Norbert Wiener, *Cybernetics: Or Control and Communication in the Animal and the Machine*, 2nd ed. (Cambridge, MA: The MIT Press, 1965), 12.

22. Lazzarato, *Puissances de l'invention*, 18; Gabriel de Tarde's *Monadologie et Sociology* was originally published in 1893, but according to Filippo Domenicali composed mostly in 1875. Domenicali argues for an esoteric Tarde that expresses itself in the monadology as "secret metaphysics," but which Tarde tended not to make so public or central for fear of going against the positivist spirit of the time. See Gabriel Tarde, *Monadology and Sociology* (1893, Melbourne: re.press, 2012); and Filippo Domenicali, "La Metafisica Segreta Di Tarde," in *Monadologia E Sociologia* (Verona: Ombre Corte, 2013); for a Tardean reading of digital networks which deploys Tarde's concept of imitation to think virality see Tony Sampson, *Virality: Contagion Theory in the Age of Networks* (Minneapolis and London: University of Minnesota Press, 2012); for a perspective on the relation between Tarde and social psychology see Lisa Blackman, "Reinventing Psychological Matters: The Importance of the Suggestive Realm in Tarde's Ontology," *Economy and Society* 36, no. 4 (2007).

23. Gilles Deleuze, *The Fold: Leibniz and the Baroque*, transl. Tom Conley (London: The Athlone Press, 1993), 23–24.

24. Gilles Deleuze, *Negotiations 1972–1990*, transl. Martin Joughin (New York: University of Columbia Press, 1995), 157–158.

25. Deleuze, *The Fold*, 25.

26. Deleuze, *The Fold*, 27.

27. Deleuze, *The Fold*, 50.

28. *Ibid.*, 27.

29. Deleuze, *Negotiations*, 158.

30. Deleuze, *The Fold*, 14.

31. Munster, *An Aesthesia of Networks*, 21.

32. Deleuze, *The Fold*, 17.

33. Deleuze, *The Fold*.

34. "Metacommunities of Code" is a collaboration between Matthew Fuller, Richard Mills, Adrian Mackenzie, Stu Sharples and Richard Mills (see http://metacommunitiesofcode.org/).

35. Deleuze, *The Fold*, 20.

36. Deleuze, *The Fold*.

37. Deleuze, *The Fold*, 18–19.

38. Deleuze, *The Fold*, 22.

39. Deleuze, *The Fold*, 24.

40. Nicholas Rescher, *G. W. Leibniz's Monadology: An Edition for Students* (London: Routledge, 2002), 45.

41. Rescher, *G. W. Leibniz's Monadology*, 71.

42. Rescher, *G. W. Leibniz's Monadology*, 87.

43. Rescher, *G. W. Leibniz's Monadology*, 91.

44. On the posthuman and the post-humanities see Rosi Braidotti, *The Posthuman* (Cambridge: Polity Press, 2013); on the return of panpsychism in contemporary philosophy and media theory see Steven Shaviro, *The Universe of Things: On Speculative Realism* (Minneapolis and London: University of Minnesota Press, 2014); on machinic animism see Angela Melitopoulos and Maurizio Lazzarato, "Assemblages: Félix Guattari and Machinic Animism," *e-flux journal* 36 (2012).

45. Tarde, *Monadology and Sociology*, 15.

46. Tarde, *Monadology and Sociology*, 26.

47. Tarde, *Monadology and Sociology*, 26–27.

48. see Benkler, *The Wealth of Networks*, 20.

49. Lazzarato, *Puissances de l'invention*, 11.

50. Lazzarato, *Puissances de l'invention*, 92.

51. Lazzarato, *Puissances de l'invention*, 97,

52. Pierre Dardot and Christian Raval, *La nouvelle raison du monde: Essai sur la société néolibérale* (Paris: Editions La Découverte, 2009), 38.

53. Tarde, *Monadology and Sociology*, 24.

54. Tarde, *Monadology and Sociology*, 24–25.

55. Tarde, *Monadology and Sociology*, 25–26.

Foreword to Project 2501: The A.I. Speech (2016)

1. See Fase 25, https://ilmanifesto.it/fase-25-aprile-2020

Acknowledgments

The essays that make up this book span the decade that goes between the late 2000s and the year 2020—a period bounded, on the one hand, by the financial crisis of 2008 and on the other, by the outbreak of the Covid19 virus. They have not been updated, that is cleansed of what might feel obsolete or old, but only subjected to minor editorial or linguistic revisions. I have chosen to present them as documents of a more general archive of the process of theorization of the development of digital inter-networking over the last two decades real time takes on different aspects of this process of subsumption as it happened. The context within which they were elaborated was that of the social study that went on in grassroots "nomad universities," squatted or "liberated" spaces run as commons, small research centers, activist research projects, and also some academic conferences. They were thus mostly conceived, elaborated, and discussed in collective spaces—predominantly in Southern Europe, but also within a wider global network of research and activism.

In these spaces and thanks to the efforts of those who struggled to seize and maintain them, I was involved in discussions and exposed to thinking that catalyzed the questions that I could ask of that which I was interested in, such as the transformation of the internet, in hopefully politically engaging ways. I owe much to those various individuals, groups and collectives who have generously labored, often under duress, to nurture and maintain viable spaces of social study, cultural expression, and political elaboration. In particular, I owe my understanding of theories of financialization, cognitive capitalism, affective labor, social cooperation, biopolitical production, the multitude, and the Common to the collectives of post-workerist inspiration which I was part of in Italy during this period.

I am grateful for all I have learned and for the possibility to think together to: the "nomad" university movement in Italy, in particular to Uninomade, Uninomade 2.0, Euronomade, but also Effimera and SCEPSI (European School for Social imagination) for constructing convivial, challenging and warm spaces of contact between theoretical thinking and activist practices; self-managed spaces such as Esc, Zero81, L'Asilo, Lo

Scugnizzo Liberato, Macao, Teatro Valle, Batterfly
and Empros for having made it possible to see the
Common at work; the Centre for Postcolonial and
Gender Studies and the Technoculture Research
Unit at L'Orientale University for being my most
immediate and intimate circle of support and
exchange; the Centre for Cultural Studies at
Goldsmiths' College, University of London, the
Rosa Luxembourg Institute in Berlin, the Institute
of Network Culture in Amsterdam, the seminar
series on Cognitive Capitalism at the Université
Paris 1 (Panthéon-Sorbonne), Robin Hood Minor
Asset Management, the Psychopathologies of
Cognitive Capitalism conferences, the Bergen
Assembly, Art is Open Source/Her Loves Data, the
Reina Sofia Museum, and the Transmediale festival
for catalyzing thinking and allowing for contacts
based in affinity; the ATACD, Immediations,
Transit Labor and Ecologie Politiche del Presente
research networks for challenging and fundamental collective intellectual elaboration; *il manifesto*
newspaper (especially the culture and technology
sections) for the indefatigable public work of information and elaboration on the relation between
capitalist development and technological innovation; and the *Theory, Culture and Society* journal
for the relentless commitment to rigorous and
challenging theoretical work which I have learned
so much from. As usual, none of these groups or

spaces should be blamed for that which this book does not account for or gets wrong.

Finally, amongst the multitude of those who contributed to the thinking that has gone into this book, a special mention goes to those who are no longer with us and whom are sorely missed, that is to Lidia, Benedetto, Couze, Ali, Sebastian and Salvatore.

ABOUT THE AUTHOR

Tiziana Terranova is an Italian theorist and activist whose work focuses on the effects of information technology on society through concepts such as digital labor and commons. She lives and works in Naples, Italy, where she is a Professor of Digital Media and Cultural Studies at "L'Orientale" University. Terranova has published the monograph *Network Culture: Politics for the Information Age* (Pluto Press, 2004).